May 8, 1988

For Yvonne and Bill —
With Love,
Kate

Wildflowers of Canada

Photographs and
introductory texts by

Tim Fitzharris

Species descriptions by

Audrey Fraggalosch

Illustrations by

Diana Thompson

Toronto
Oxford University Press
1986

To Pat

Canadian Cataloguing in Publication Data

Fitzharris, Tim, 1948–
    Wildflowers of Canada

Includes indexes.
ISBN 0-19-540566-8

1. Wild flowers — Canada.   2. Wild flowers —
Canada — Identification.   I. Title.

QK201.F58 1986   582.13'0971   C86-094240-6

Text and photographs © Tim Fitzharris 1986
Line drawings © Diana Thompson
OXFORD is a trademark of Oxford University Press
1 2 3 4 - 9 8 7 6
Printed and Bound in Canada by
Friesen Printers Ltd.
Altona, Manitoba, Canada R0G 0B0

Contents

Preface

From fragile glacier lilies strewn over a Rocky Mountain ridge to tough, heavy-trunked silver maples towering more than ten storeys out of an Ontario swamp, thousands of varieties of flowering plants enrich the Canadian landscape. The obvious economic importance of some woody species aside, the value of wild plants for most of us lies in their aesthetic appeal. Bikers, canoeists, fishermen, and birdwatchers all know the beauty of wildflowers — a still glade suddenly illuminated by the glow of a trillium; a meadow splashed with rainbow bouquets of blue iris, devil's paintbrush, and ox-eye daisy; an entire vista washed with the pastel hues of mustard or camas. We need not be botanists for wildflowers to lure us deep into the ghostly bog, launch us up a steep alpine trail, or guide our footsteps through a burgeoning spring forest.

But we would be wrong to think that a wildflower's beauty was intended for us. Long before people appeared on the planet, plants were developing ways to attract insects, those airborne messengers that so efficiently carry the fertilizing pollen from one flower to the next. The insects were enticed by the flowers' exotic shapes and colours, their intoxicating perfumes and savoury nectars. And the wildflowers fed more than the butterflies and bees. Their fruits fattened the bears and refuelled the migrating thrushes and waxwings, while their stems and leaves sustained the giant herds of deer, elk, mountain sheep, and moose that once roamed the continent.

This book pays tribute both to wildflowers' sensual appeal and to their ecological worth. Above all, we hope it arouses enthusiasm among its readers — beginning and seasoned botanists alike — so that their voices may add reasoned volume to the plea for conservation. If they help to throw even one grain of sand into the military-industrial machine that each day grinds more of the earth into chrome, plastic, pesticides, and missiles, our efforts will prove to be not only enjoyable, but honourable.

I would like to thank Dr R.T. Ogilvie, Curator of Botany at the British Columbia Provincial Museum, for his careful and thorough scientific review of the text, illustrations, and photographs.

I am also grateful to my two colleagues in this venture, Diana Thompson for her exquisitely rendered drawings and Audrey Fraggalosch for her concise, well-researched text.

Further appreciation is extended to friends and associates who provided assistance with photographs in the field: Don Li-Leger, David Tomlinson, Jim Fitzharris, Erma Fitzharris, Patrick Fitzharris, Colin Knecht, Lang Elliott, Richard and Judy Bonney, and especially Audrey Fraggalosch.

Tim Fitzharris

Introduction

For most people the primary appeal of wildflowers is their beauty. However, as we have tried to show in this book, these plants offer much more to discover and enjoy. They are presented here in three ways. The photographic plates give impressions of the colour and shape of each species, usually in magnified form. The line drawings are more definitive, revealing the entire structure and growth habit to aid in field identification. The text highlights interesting characteristics and functions, defines growing conditions and range, and points out various details of ecology and plant lore. (The few botanical terms that are used are all explained in the Glossary.)

Only a fraction of the thousands of species found in Canada are represented here. They are arranged according to the habitat where they are usually found, although some highly adapted species could easily have been included in more than one section (this is usually noted in the text). The habitat categories are obviously broad, but for the novice they provide a good basis for learning the relationship between environment and a plant's structure and behaviour. Knowing when and where you are likely to find it in bloom will improve your chances of seeing any flower — even the rarer species — in the wild.

Form and Function

To understand and enjoy the lives of wildflowers to the fullest, it helps to know the

Ox-eye daisies toss in the summer wind.

The Parts of a Flower

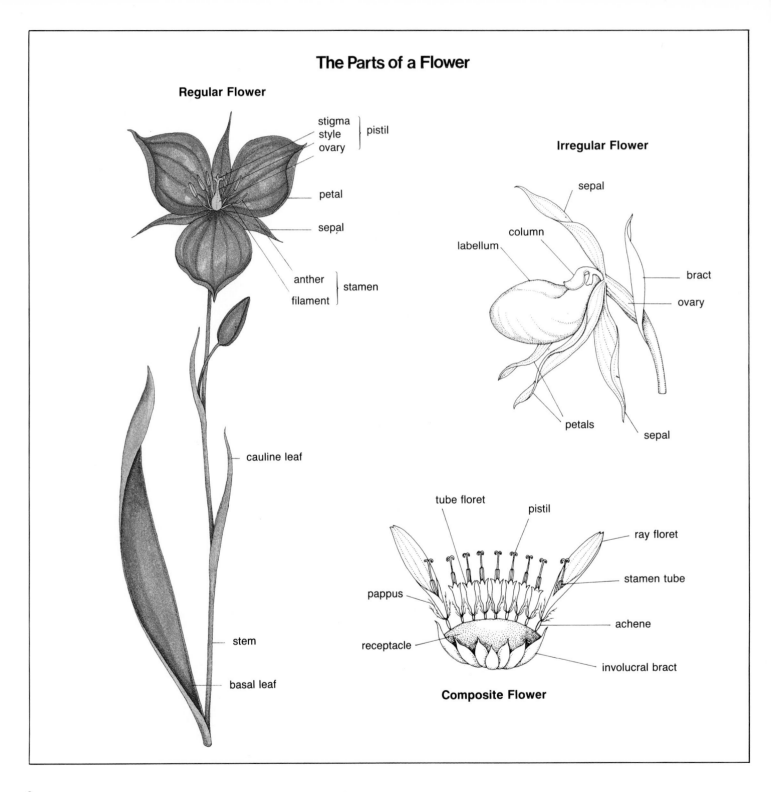

Regular Flower

stigma
style — pistil
ovary

petal

sepal

anther
filament — stamen

cauline leaf

stem

basal leaf

Irregular Flower

sepal

column
labellum

bract

ovary

petals

sepal

tube floret

pistil

ray floret

stamen tube

pappus

achene

receptacle

involucral bract

Composite Flower

basic parts of plants and their major functions. The following is a brief outline.

Roots, the plant's main providers of food, absorb water and nutrients from the soil. They come in two basic types. Thick, tubular tap roots grow straight down into the soil to a depth where the moisture content is fairly steady and dependable. Fibrous roots are numerous and much finer, growing in a tangled mass near the surface, where they can soak up the more variable water supply available at this level. Although many plants enjoy a combination of these two root systems, one generally gains dominance as a result of various environmental factors.

In addition, roots serve to anchor and support the plant's stem. They may also function as food reservoirs — a good example is the carrot. Some root systems are so dense that they prevent other plants from becoming established nearby, thus ensuring a greater supply of food and moisture for themselves; others emit toxins to limit competition from rival species. Finally, many plants have specialized underground stems, called rhizomes, that grow laterally, allowing the plant to spread by sending up new stems and leaves.

The stem is one of the plant's largest and strongest parts, containing the pipelines that carry food and water to and from the leaves and roots. It also supports the leaves and flowers in such a way that they can perform their tasks most efficiently. The leaves must be arrayed to maximize their absorption of sunlight, while the flower must be positioned so that it catches the wind or advertises its presence to insects in order for pollination to occur; then the fruit must be served up for birds or breezes that will disperse the seeds. The stem must make sure that flower and leaf do not interfere with

each other's vital functions, and in so doing it demonstrates some ingenious solutions to the problems of spatial arrangement.

The leaf is the plant's production centre. Each one acts as a sunlight receptor, using this energy to link up carbon dioxide and water to produce carbohydrates through the process of photosynthesis, the basis for all life on earth. A quick examination of any patch of woodland or meadow will reveal an amazing variety of leaf structures and shapes. These configurations are competitive. Each variation is intended to gain a unique advantage for the particular species, enabling it to receive more sunlight than its neighbour while simultaneously limiting the damaging effects of drying winds or hungry predators. In the shaded forest understorey most leaves spread flat to catch as much of the weak light as possible, while on the sun-baked prairies many herbs have slim, upright leaves, to avoid overheating and dessication. In some species, such as the dandelion, the leaves spread out to cover adjacent plants, cutting off their light and eventually claiming their territory. In others the leaves are covered with tiny hairs or wax to retain moisture, or prickles or poison to thwart insects or mammals looking for a meal.

The job of flowers is reproduction. Their evolutionary development has been closely linked to the insect world: almost all floral structures are designed to entice insects to deliver the sperm-laden pollen to specific female targets. (A more primitive system, still practised by the conifers, relies on the indiscriminate energy of the wind to transport the male sex cells; naturally most are blown in the wrong direction, forcing the plant to produce enough to make up for what at times becomes a tremendous waste.) Attracted by scent and bright col-

ours, insects are directed along the flower's specially marked pathways and tunnels to reach the nourishing reward of pollen and nectar. Along the way they may be brushed, whacked, or even pummelled by the stamens and pistils. In the process pollen is loaded onto or unloaded from their bodies, usually in a sequence designed to favour cross-pollination.

The flowers of some plants — especially those in open terrain, like the grasses — are small and plain and, as you would suspect, achieve pollination by the wind. A design consideration evident in the colour and shape of the blossoms of some species is the need to collect and absorb heat energy from the sun, the extra warmth increasing nectar production.

Most blooms have four parts. The sepals are leaf-like sheaths, usually green, that encase the bloom while it is still developing. Petals make up the colourful inner ring of leaf-like parts that serve to attract pollinators to the reproductive organs usually found in the centre of the blossom. The female organ, the pistil, consists of an egg enclosed in an ovary from which projects a tube called the style. The style terminates in a special tip, the stigma, which receives the male sex cells, or pollen. Usually several in number, the stamens are the male parts. They may be located on the same bloom as the pistil or on a separate flower containing only male parts. Each stamen consists of a stalk, the filament, tipped with a pollen-producing structure called the anther.

The reproductive process begins once pollen is deposited on the stigma. The pollen grows down inside the style until it reaches the ovary, where it releases its precious cargo of sperm into the egg to initiate the development of the seed. The surrounding ovary grows into the fruit — soft and fleshy like an apple or thin and tough like wheat.

Cross-pollination occurs when sperm from one plant combines with the egg of another to create an entirely new and unique genetic combination. In some cases this may produce a hybrid species or even initiate an evolutionary process that could eventually yield a new species. For example, the result could be a plant with a longer tap-root or a tougher stem — characteristics likely to be favoured by natural selection. Self-pollination, which yields seed-producing plants essentially like the parent, inhibits the spe-

cies' adaptation to the stresses or opportunities of a changing environment. To prevent self-pollination, certain highly evolved species produce blooms with ingenious mechanisms and pathways that serve to load the insect with pollen only when it is leaving the blossom. Others simply separate the pistils and stamens by growing plants with either male or female flowers, but not both. Others still grow both sexual parts but time the development of the stamens to occur after the ovary has been fertilized by some outside source.

To ensure that the insect couriers don't deliver the pollen to the wrong place (daisy pollen is wasted on a thistle), flowers of the same species all manufacture nectar at about the same time each day. Insects and hummingbirds are programmed to benefit from the strategy, and they waste little time visiting blooms when they are not producing. Once fertilized, some flowers signal the pollinators that they are no longer producing nectar by changing their shape, colour, odour, or taste.

A ladybird beetle emerges from a dandelion.

Collecting Wildflowers

The earth's natural communities are diminishing at an ever increasing rate. Thus for philosophical, if not practical, reasons, collecting or transplanting wild flora is not a sound practice. In fact, it's not too different from saving chipmunk skins or caging a peregrine falcon. Although these activities are widespread and have some educational merit, there are less harmful ways of enjoying and learning about wildflowers. Some of them are outlined below.

Field Observations

First of all, try examining each flower carefully while you are in the field. Don't just give it a quick whiff or an admiring glance and repeat its names under your breath. If you carry a hand lens you can examine the specimen in magnification. Try to identify the various parts and their functions. However strange the configuration of a blossom may be, it's rewarding to be able to trace its origins back to the four basic components (sepals, petals, pistil, and stamens) and to speculate on the advantages it has gained because of its modifications. Scrutinize the leaves and stems, giving special attention to their shape, colour, and texture. How are such features unique? How do they relate to the special niche the plant occupies in its environment? Carry a field guide and, if possible, make a special note of the features that distinguish the genus and species of a particular specimen, as well as those that allow the plant to be grouped with other related species into a family.

Keep a wildflower journal for your observations. Record any aspect of plant life that

Camouflaged to blend in with its surroundings, a crab spider ambushes a fly.

you find worthwhile—physical dimensions, shape, colour, flowering date, blooming duration, fruit production, soil and moisture conditions, behavioural features, special structural adaptations to wind, rain, sun, predation, pollination, and so on. Perhaps you would like to investigate some aspect of floral natural history in detail—methods of seed dispersal, a particular family, population studies, hybrids, consumption by wildlife. There are many areas of botany, particularly in the field of plant behaviour, that institutional science has yet to explore. Generally no special equipment or skill is needed—just a strong curiosity and an urge to observe and understand natural phenomena. In any case, the more effort you give your investigation, the greater will be both your enjoyment and the chances for true and valuable scientific discovery.

Many enthusiasts express their interest in wildflowers by sketching or painting. Some use the sketch pad simply to clarify or add to their field notes, while others make drawings that are valuable in their own right as works of art. Field sketches may become the basis for more elaborate works completed in the studio, with all the thematic considerations of fine art. There are several ways of getting started, from private study to courses and workshops. Many a lifetime has been spent in botanical art and illustration, contributing greatly to both art and science.

Photography

No doubt one of the most popular and, ultimately, most challenging ways to enjoy wildflowers is to photograph them. A wildflower snapshot makes a pleasant souvenir, and it's fun and easy to take. However, a snapshot seldom communicates the sensual

A swallowtail butterfly draws nectar from a bull thistle.

pleasure the photographer felt in making the picture, nor is it likely to show the wildflower's important characteristics with adequate clarity. Dramatic, definitive portraits require considerable skill and effort. Fortunately, the technical principles are easy to understand and apply, and the special equipment required need not be expensive.

The 35-mm single-lens-reflex camera is by far the best choice for photographing wildflowers. Although the normal lens usually sold with the camera is fine and widely used, you will need lenses of other focal lengths for special effects. A telephoto lens, for example, will seem to compress or concentrate more blossoms within the field of view, while a wide-angle lens will tend to expand or increase the apparent distance between individual flowers or between flowers and background. For adequate magnification of the subject, a device is needed to allow the lens to focus more closely than normal. A close-up supplementary lens (built like an ordinary lens filter) is a simple and inexpensive tool for this purpose; a lens extension device is more versatile and produces better images, but it is more expensive. More serious wildflower photographers will want to use a macro lens, a special-purpose optic designed for working with small subjects. Most reputable camera retailers can give you competent advice on selecting equipment.

Colour slide film is the best type to use. It is the least expensive and produces results of the highest quality. Not only can the images be projected for the benefit of a number of people, but they can be made into prints of excellent detail and brilliance. A medium film speed (ISO 50–100) is recommended, as it accurately records nature's subtle hues and intricate structures and yet is sensitive enough for use in the low light levels frequently encountered when shooting wildflowers.

Because of the high degree of magnification required to photograph wildflowers, even the slightest movement of the camera during exposure will cause an unacceptable loss of sharpness. The most effective and convenient solution is a tripod that is able to position the camera close to the ground. The most useful model allows you to remove the centre column and reinsert it upside down, so that the camera hangs between the legs. Sometimes beanbags — in a pinch, rocks or branches — will do as ground-level supports (I once pressed into service two apples and a ham and cheese on rye). To maintain absolute steadiness during the exposure, keep your hands away from the camera by tripping the shutter with a cable release. Try to release the shutter when the air is still — wind that causes the blossoms to sway or vibrate at the moment of exposure will also destroy the detail of your picture.

No matter how good your equipment is, however, the key to effective wildflower photography is light. Natural illumination, as opposed to an electronic flash, will produce the most consistent and pleasing results. It's usually advisable to arrange the lighting so that detail is retained in both the highlight and shadow areas. Overcast, hazy skies supply the soft, even light that is ideal for wildflower photography. When shooting under the harsh light of direct sun, try holding home-made reflectors of white paper or crumpled aluminum foil close to the subject, to bounce light into the shadows and bring the illumination levels into closer balance.

You can choose to light the subject from the front, the back, or the side; the choice depends on your artistic intentions. Translucent petals and leaves work well with backlight. Sidelight brings out interesting textures and shapes, while frontlight generally produces the greatest colour saturation.

The design of any wildflower photograph will be determined by the photographer's purpose and personal artistic taste. A focal length can be selected to include more or less background. Camera angle may be changed so that a pattern of twigs or a sweep of blossoms becomes more evident. Lighting can be controlled to accentuate important elements by illuminating them more brightly. An aperture may be selected to produce a depth of field that renders important components in sharp definition and distractive elements as out-of-focus blurs. The photographer can incorporate natural patterns and rhythmic flows of lines and shapes that will lead the viewer's eye through the design in an organized, directed fashion. In other words, the composition of a wildflower picture may be shaped in many ways. The only restriction is the photographer's imagination.

To learn more about photographing wildflowers you may consult reference books, take courses, or join a camera club. The amount of effort you take with your photography will be readily apparent in the images you produce. The higher the quality, the more satisfying your pictures will be to you, and the more effectively you can use them to promote the value of wild flora.

Woodland

Vast tracts of the Canadian landscape are covered with forests. The particular character of each tree community, and of the flowering shrubs and herbs that grow in its understorey, is the result of many interrelated factors: climate, soil type, land form, forest-fire occurrence. Most forests are dominated by coniferous species. On the wet Pacific coast grow dark, towering, moss-draped forests of giant Douglas fir, western hemlock, Sitka spruce, and western red cedar. The rugged mountains and valleys of the British Columbia interior are covered with less impressive stands of pines, Douglas fir, alpine fir, and Engelmann spruce. To the north, stretching nearly from coast to coast, is a vast, often monotonous expanse of spruces, tamarack, aspen, and birch known as the boreal forest. Most of the densely settled regions of Ontario, Quebec, and the Maritimes are covered with mixed coniferous and deciduous woodlands of balsam fir, pine, maple, birch, and oak. Even Ontario's deep south, extensively farmed today, was once overgrown with hardwoods—beech, maple, hickory, oak, and walnut.

Particularly in dense, moist coniferous forests, many flowering shrubs and herbs show adaptations to life in the shaded understorey. To entice insects, plants like queen's cup and single delight have glowing white or pastel blooms, heavily scented to attract insect pollinators in the dim, still atmosphere. The leaves of devil's club and trailing arbutus are broad and tinted a deep green

—the result of abundant chlorophyll—to achieve maximum photosynthetic benefit from the faint sunlight that filters through the canopy. Vines like orange honeysuckle climb as high as 6 metres to reach brighter, more exposed locations. Indian pipe, on the other hand, does not compete for light at all: lacking chlorophyll, this ghostly flower finds sustenance in the humus of the forest floor through an association with fungus. The evergreen needles of the conifers form strongly acidic surface soils, and many of the plants adapted to these conditions grow in a symbiotic relationship with a fungus that assists in nutrient uptake. In addition to Indian pipe, they include many members of the heather family and related species such as blueberries, huckleberries, cranberries, salal, and the wintergreens.

Light is not so limited in the mixed woodlands of central and eastern Canada, particularly in the spring before the leaves of the deciduous trees have unfurled. Fuelled by food stored in their roots, many perennials—trilliums, yellow trout lilies, hepaticas, spring beauties—emerge from the litter of the forest floor ahead of other plants to take advantage of the spring sun. The rising buds of bloodroot, another spring pioneer, are protected from the cold in the early stages of development by an envelope of leaves. Foremost, perhaps, among the hardy early-spring wildflowers is the skunk cabbage. Insulated by spongy leaves, it literally melts its way through winter's lingering snows with heat generated by its own res-

piration, which also speeds up the growth of the flower buds and releases aromas to attract insect pollinators. By summer the broad-leaved tree canopy is like an umbrella, and on the darkened forest floor only a glimmer remains of the blooming display that enlivened the spring woods.

Relatively few flowering plants have adapted to the cold temperatures and poorly drained, acidic soils of the northern boreal forests. Pink lady's slipper, twinflower, and bunchberry are all the more welcome in this trackless wilderness. And, though dwarfed by the cold temperatures and short growing season, blueberry proliferates, gracing the often monotonous green expanses with its creamy bell-like flowers, frosty blue fruits, and fiery autumn foliage.

Few birds or mammals would be able to make the forest their home were it not for the flowering shrubs and herbs of the understorey. This tangle of leaves and stems offers protective cover for large mammals such as deer and elk, nocturnal grazers of open terrain that prefer to remain hidden during the daylight hours. The understorey also serves as a nursery for many birds and mammals, concealing the vulnerable young from predators and shielding them from both storms and broiling sun. The nutritious foliage and fruits of understorey plants—roses, gooseberries, blueberries, blackberries, dogwoods—are a primary food source for many birds as well as squirrels, chipmunks, and bears.

Red-flowering Currant

Ribes sanguineum
GROSSULARIACEAE (GOOSEBERRY FAMILY)

This early-blooming deciduous shrub heralds the arrival of spring on the west coast. Seldom exceeding 1.5 metres in height, red-flowering currant is distinguished by its clusters of drooping red flowers and its coarsely toothed maple-like leaves. The sky-blue berries are considered edible but not choice.

HABITAT/RANGE: Many currant and gooseberry species belonging to the genus *Ribes* thrive in woodlands across Canada. Red-flowering currant is found at low elevations in southwestern British Columbia.

NOTES: Although the specific name *sanguineum* means 'blood-red', the hue varies in intensity from pink to crimson. The blooming period begins in March and coincides with the arrival of the first migrant hummingbirds, which are attracted to the brilliant colours.

◁ Rufous hummingbirds feed regularly on the nectar of red-flowering currant in the early spring.

Herb Robert
Geranium robertianum
GERANIACEAE (GERANIUM FAMILY)

A member of the geranium family, herb Robert brightens rocky woodlands with its delicate pink blooms and distinctive fern-like leaves. The deep magenta nectar lines on the five unnotched petals guide insects to the nectar source at the centre of the flower. After blooming in early summer, the flower matures into a seed pod with a shape that gives this plant its other common name — crane's bill.

HABITAT/RANGE: Growing in areas of partial shade, herb Robert is native to Europe but thrives in woodlands from southern Ontario to the Maritimes. A number of similar wild geraniums are found across Canada.

NOTES: The seeds of wild geraniums are eaten by some songbirds and rodents. Moose and white-tailed deer occasionally browse on the leaves.

Common Wood Sorrel

Oxalis montana

OXALIDACEAE (WOOD SORREL FAMILY)

This dainty herb, like other members of its family, is distinguished by three clover-like leaflets shaped like inverted hearts. The slender stems of common wood sorrel each bear a solitary flower in early summer. The bloom consists of five white petals delicately veined with pink.

HABITAT/RANGE: Several species of wood sorrel are found in moist, rich woodlands across eastern Canada.

NOTES: Rabbits and deer occasionally feed on wood sorrel's succulent leaflets. Slate-coloured juncos and savannah sparrows eat the minute seeds.

Pacific Dogwood
Cornus nuttallii
CORNACEAE (DOGWOOD FAMILY)

British Columbians had good reason to choose Pacific dogwood as their provincial flower. This small deciduous tree blooms each year from April to June, and sometimes again in the fall. Often mistaken for petals are the large white floral leaves that radiate from a pin-cushion-like cluster containing the true flowers. By fall these small greenish blooms mature into bead-like red berries. The glossy opposite leaves display the characteristic dogwood veins, which curve parallel to the leaf edge.

HABITAT/RANGE: Dogwoods are found from coast to coast. Pacific dogwood occurs on the west coast, flowering dogwood (*Cornus florida*) in the east, and red-osier dogwood (*C. stolonifera*) across Canada.

NOTES: There are approximately fifty species of dogwoods in the world. Except for the flowering and Pacific dogwoods, which attain the stature of small trees, all are shrubs.

Calypso Orchid

Calypso bulbosa
ORCHIDACEAE (ORCHID FAMILY)

This nymph of the woodlands is a fragrant representative of the large and varied orchid family. A solitary pink flower and a single parallel-veined oval leaf are its distinguishing features. The only member of its genus in North America, it is unfortunately becoming increasingly rare.

HABITAT/RANGE: The calypso orchid is found across Canada in moist coniferous forests, where it is often hidden among mosses.

NOTES: Orchid flowers are characterized by a structure known as the column, formed by the fusion of some of the stamens with the style and stigma.

Orange Honeysuckle

Lonicera ciliosa
CAPRIFOLIACEAE (HONEYSUCKLE FAMILY)

In their search for sunlight, the long trailing stems of orange honeysuckle twist themselves tightly around a variety of shrubs and trees. This woody vine is particularly conspicuous in May and June, when its clusters of trumpet-shaped orange flowers are in bloom. The flower stems grow directly through the centre of a pair of fused oval leaves.

HABITAT/RANGE: Many species of honeysuckle are found in woodlands across Canada. Orange honeysuckle is restricted to southern British Columbia.

NOTES: Hummingbirds and swallowtail butterflies are attracted to the bright orange flowers, reaching the nectar with their long extensible tongues and probosces.

Northern Bush Honeysuckle

Diervilla lonicera
CAPRIFOLIACEAE (HONEYSUCKLE FAMILY)

This low-lying shrub is distinguished from other members of the honeysuckle family by its finely toothed leaves. The funnel-shaped yellow flowers usually occur in threes at the tip of the spreading branches. The more deeply coloured lower lobe of the flower serves as a landing platform for insects.

Blooming in early summer, the bush often swarms with bees drawing nectar from the blossoms.

HABITAT/RANGE: Northern bush honeysuckle ranges from Manitoba to Newfoundland, preferring open woods and dry soils.

NOTES: The honeysuckle family consists mainly of woody vines and shrubs characterized by opposite leaves and tubular flowers.

Spiderwort

Tradescantia virginiana
COMMELINACEAE
(SPIDERWORT FAMILY)

A terminal cluster of violet flowers with hairy sepals distinguishes this plant from other members of its family. The three roundish petals, which appear in early summer, are accented by golden stamens. Like other spiderworts, it has two long leaf-like bracts below the flower cluster. The drooping grass-like leaves are folded lengthwise, forming a channel where rainwater can run off.

HABITAT/RANGE: Thriving in moist woods and meadows, spiderwort is found in southern Ontario and Quebec.

NOTES: The genus *Tradescantia* is named for John Tradescant, gardener to Charles I. A similar species, Ohio spiderwort (*T. ohiensis*) produces pink and white as well as violet blossoms.

Virginia Waterleaf

Hydrophyllum virginianum
HYDROPHYLLACEAE
(WATERLEAF FAMILY)

In early spring you can recognize this annual by its loose terminal cluster of delicate bell-shaped flowers made up of white or pale violet petals with long protruding stamens. The irregular shape of the five to seven lobed leaves is another distinguishing feature.

HABITAT/RANGE: Preferring rich soils, Virginia waterleaf is found from Manitoba to Quebec. Similar species include appendaged waterleaf (*Hydrophyllum appendiculatum*), which grows in southern Ontario, and woollen breeches (*H. capitatum*), a rare species occasionally found in exposed areas of the southern Rockies.

NOTES: The generic name *Hydrophyllum*, meaning 'water leaf', probably refers to the mottled pattern that makes the leaves appear waterstained.

Blue-eyed Mary

Collinsia grandiflora

SCROPHULARIACEAE (FIGWORT FAMILY)

Like other members of the figwort family, blue-eyed Mary has five petals joined into a tube that is divided at the top into two lips, the upper one consisting of two petals and the lower one of three. The pale mauve of the upper lip contrasts vividly with the royal blue of the lower. The plant's lower leaves grow opposite on the thin stem, while the upper ones occur in small whorls. This dainty annual blooms and sets seed all within a few weeks in April and May.

HABITAT/RANGE: Perhaps the most common spring wildflower on the west coast, blue-eyed Mary flourishes in a variety of soils. It favours forest openings and dry exposed areas.

NOTES: The generic name *Collinsia* honours an early American botanist, Zacheus Collins.

Pink Lady's Slipper

Cypripedium acaule
ORCHIDACEAE (ORCHID FAMILY)

Humans are not the only species attracted to the colourful scented pouch of this wild orchid. Bees enter the front of the heavily veined pink lip and crawl up towards the top of the slipper, pollinating the flower in the process. As a bee exits, its back is brushed with pollen from the anthers, preparing it to fertilize the next flower it visits. This ingenious process maximizes the chances for cross-pollination among species.

HABITAT/RANGE: Several lady's-slipper species are found across Canada, with the pink the most common and widespread. It ranges from Manitoba to Newfoundland and thrives in the acidic soils of coniferous forests.

NOTES: Pink lady's slipper is the floral emblem of Prince Edward Island.

Indian Pipe

Monotropa uniflora
PYROLACEAE (WINTERGREEN
FAMILY)

This ghostly member of the wintergreen
family pokes its translucent stems through
the forest floor in early summer. The waxy
pipes crowned by nodding white flower buds
lack chlorophyll and bear clasping, scale-like
leaves. Compounding its eerie qualities,
Indian pipe will turn black if touched, and
eventually the whole plant darkens with age.

HABITAT/RANGE: Indian pipe is found
across Canada in the deep shade of coniferous forests.

NOTE: This species was long thought to be
a saprophyte—a plant that feeds on dead or
decaying organic matter. It has since been
established that Indian pipe is in fact a
parasite. Unable to manufacture its own
food, it feeds directly off another living
plant.

Salmonberry

Rubus spectabilis
ROSACEAE (ROSE FAMILY)

Salmonberry is most conspicuous in early spring, when its magenta flowers begin blooming before the raspberry-like leaflets have fully opened. Armed with scattered weak spines along its reddish-brown stems, this tall deciduous shrub produces fruit by early summer. The blooming period is so long that flowers and fruit can sometimes be found on the same bush. The tart berries ripen to either a ruby red or a salmon colour.

HABITAT/RANGE: *Rubus* is a common genus across Canada and is represented by many species. Salmonberry is restricted to the Pacific rain forest of British Columbia, often forming large thickets in moist bottomlands, woods, and clearings.

NOTES: The sprouts and berries of this plant were collected in large quantities by all Coast Indian groups. Picked in spring, the sprouts were peeled and eaten either raw or steamed. The juicy berries, too juicy to be dried, were usually eaten fresh.

A black bear visits a salmonberry patch.

Satin-Flower

Sisyrinchium douglasii
IRIDACEAE (IRIS FAMILY)

Satin-flower is one of the first species to bloom every year, opening its exquisite reddish-purple flowers as early as February. Dangling from the centre of the satiny petals are three brilliant yellow anthers and a prominent pistil. Another common name for this species is 'grass widow' — a reference to the fact that the nodding flowers wither a day or two after blooming, leaving behind a spray of grass-like leaves.

HABITAT/RANGE: Although a number of *Sisyrinchium* species are found in open woodlands and dry meadows across Canada, satin-flower bears the largest bloom in the genus (about 4 centimetres across). Its range is restricted to southwestern British Columbia, particularly Vancouver Island.

NOTES: The specific name *douglasii* honours David Douglas, a nineteenth-century English botanist and explorer who travelled widely in western Canada and collected many plants. He discovered this species on the Columbia River, east of Portland, Oregon.

Indian Plum

Osmaronia cerasiformis
ROSACEAE (ROSE FAMILY)

This tall deciduous shrub is the first to bloom each spring on the west coast. Racemes of four to nine drooping white flowers hang from the upright leaf clusters. Both the flowers and the prominently veined elliptical leaves exude a pungent odour, giving this species its other common name: skunk bush. The plum-like berries ripen to a dark blue by early summer.

HABITAT/RANGE: Indian plum is restricted to the southern coast of British Columbia, where it is commonly found around the edge of forests.

NOTES: The small, bitter berries are relished by birds and were eaten in small quantities by Coast Indian groups.

Single Delight

Moneses uniflora
PYROLACEAE (WINTERGREEN FAMILY)

As if suspended in mid-air, the solitary bloom of single delight lends an ethereal beauty to mossy woodlands. The delicately scented flower blooms throughout the summer, displaying a prominently sculptured pistil at the centre of its waxy ivory petals. The slender stem rises from a basal rosette of shiny evergreen leaves.

HABITAT/RANGE: Single delight thrives in moist forests, often on moss-covered ground or nurse logs. It occurs in woodlands across Canada, from sea level to 2,000 metres.

NOTES: The wintergreen family, to which single delight belongs, is made up of low herbaceous perennials with evergreen basal leaves and nodding flowers.

Big-Leaf Maple

Acer macrophyllum
ACERACEAE (MAPLE FAMILY)

Big-leaf maple is the largest and fastest-growing maple in western Canada, sometimes reaching heights of 30 metres. It also produces the biggest leaf of any Canadian maple, 15 to 25 centimetres in length and featuring five prominent lobes. Clusters of greenish-yellow flowers appear as the leaves unfold, exuding a sweet fragrance into the spring air. In fall the ripe seeds float down in paired wings through the golden foliage.

HABITAT/RANGE: Ten different species of maple, Canada's national tree, occur across the country. Big-leaf maple is confined to the coast forest and wet interior of British Columbia, where it thrives in moist soils.

NOTES: Maple seeds, buds, and flowers provide food for many birds and animals. Squirrels and chipmunks eat the seeds, and birds commonly use the leaves and seed stalks in their nests.

29

Yellow Trout Lily

Erythronium americanum
LILIACEAE (LILY FAMILY)

With its protruding pistil shaped like an adder's tongue, this is one of spring's most flamboyant wildflowers. Like other members of the *Erythronium* genus, yellow trout lily usually produces a solitary nodding flower with six tepals. Mottled brown leaves complement the bright yellow bloom.

HABITAT/RANGE: Preferring moist woods, yellow trout lily ranges from southern Ontario to the Maritimes. A similar eastern species, white trout lily (*E. albinum*), bears a white flower.

NOTES: After a lily flower has been pollinated, its tepals curve upwards to reveal the stamens and anthers. This is thought to be a signal to insects to pass the flower by, as it has already been fertilized and no longer produces nectar.

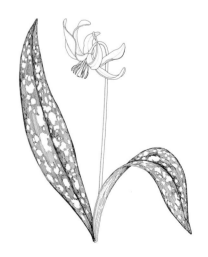

Red Trillium

Trillium erectum
LILIACEAE (LILY FAMILY)

No flowers are more familiar in the eastern woodlands than the trilliums. This species has the characteristic trillium flower consisting of three large petal-like bracts and three sepals borne above a whorl of leaves. However, the attractive red flower has a distinctly unpleasant smell, which has given rise to other common names for the plant: stinking Benjamin and wet-dog trillium.

The foul odour is thought to attract carrion flies, which pollinate the flower.

HABITAT/RANGE: Red trillium ranges throughout eastern Canada, thriving in moist, shady woodlands.

NOTES: After the trillium's seed pods burst open, ants collect the seeds, which contain oil in little appendages called strophioles. The ants eat the strophioles but leave the seeds intact. They have been known to carry trillium seeds as far as 9 metres from the parent plant.

32

Prickly Rose

Rosa acicularis

ROSACEAE (ROSE FAMILY)

The large pink blossoms of prickly rose bloom all summer long. The beetles in this photograph are among the insects that use the flower's soft, spreading petals and golden stamens as a mating platform. Like other wild roses, the prickly rose has stems armed with stiff prickles that guard its leaflets, flowers and, eventually, fruit, or rose hips.

HABITAT/RANGE: Wild roses perfume woodlands and fields across Canada. Prickly rose is particularly abundant in Alberta, where it is the provincial flower.

NOTES: The fleshy exterior of the fruit and the hairy seeds have considerable food value for wildlife. Thickets of wild roses also make excellent nesting areas for birds and provide protective cover for many small mammals.

◁ A red squirrel feeds on a rose hip.

33

Snowberry

Symphoricarpos albus
CAPRIFOLIACEAE (HONEYSUCKLE FAMILY)

No matter what the time of year, this shrub presents some eye-catching feature. In summer its minute, bell-shaped pink flowers cluster near the end of the slender twigs. These mature into soft clumps of waxy white berries that last well into winter, when many other deciduous shrubs have lost both foliage and fruit. The thin opposite leaves are roughly oval in shape.

HABITAT/RANGE: Snowberry grows along roadsides and in open woods and clearings. Also known as waxberry, this genus is represented by several close relatives across Canada.

NOTES: Snowberry fruits are a staple winter food for many gamebirds, including grouse, which eat the seeds and then deposit them intact in their droppings, spreading the shrub widely.

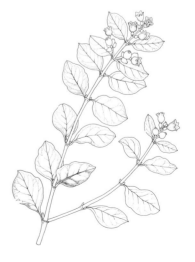

Bitter Cherry

Prunus emarginata
ROSACEAE (ROSE FAMILY)

In spring bitter cherry trees burst with flowers and fragrance. The rounded clusters of small white blooms first appear when the leaves are almost half grown. By midsummer the flowers have matured into pea-sized bright red berries. On the Pacific coast bitter cherry can be identified by a dense coating of hairs on the underside of its narrow, tapered leaves and flower stalks. Also distinctive is the shiny reddish-brown bark of mature specimens, which is marked by powdery orange stripes called lenticels.

HABITAT/RANGE: Wild cherry trees grow all across Canada, thriving in moist sparsely wooded areas. Bitter cherry's range is restricted to the southern half of British Columbia.

NOTES: Wild cherries are among the most important foods for both gamebirds and songbirds, which swallow the fruit and regurgitate the pits. Chipmunks and deer mice often feed on fruit that has fallen to the ground. Deer, elk, moose, and rabbits will also browse on the twigs, foliage, and bark.

Western Trillium

Trillium ovatum
LILIACEAE (LILY FAMILY)

A number of trilliums, including the western species, are also known by the name of
wake-robin, because of their early blooming
period. Three large veined leaves form a
whorl under the large white flower. Once it
has been pollinated, the petals change colour
from white to pink or dark purple — as a
signal to insects that it has already been
fertilized.

HABITAT/RANGE: The trillium genus is
represented by several species across Canada.
Western trillium is found mainly in coastal
British Columbia, with sporadic occurrences in woodlands in the interior of the
province.

NOTES: It takes a minimum of six years
under good conditions for a white trillium
to produce its first bloom from seed. *Trillium grandiflorum*, the showiest species, is
the provincial flower of Ontario.

Bunchberry

Cornus canadensis
CORNACEAE (DOGWOOD FAMILY)

This dwarf dogwood carpets the forest floor with its showy blooms and lush foliage. Rising above a whorl of distinctly parallel-veined leaves are four large, white, petal-like bracts (modified leaves). They surround the real flowers, which form a dense cluster of greenish blooms at the centre of the plant. Bunchberry flowers in early summer and by August produces bunches of bright red berries.

HABITAT/RANGE: Bunchberry thrives in damp coniferous woods across Canada, ranging as far north as southern Greenland. Tolerant of low light conditions, this robust perennial is common throughout the vast boreal forest of northern Canada.

NOTES: The sweet berries are relished by a number of songbirds, particularly vireos.

White Fawn Lily

Erythronium oregonum
LILIACEAE (LILY FAMILY)

A favourite springtime sport for flower-chasers on the west coast is to discover the first fawn lily in bloom. Flowering in April, this graceful perennial usually produces only one blossom, although doubles and trebles are common in rich soils. Each elegant flower consists of six white tepals curving backwards to display the golden anthers and prominent pistil. Almost as showy as the flowers are the two large mottled leaves.

HABITAT/RANGE: A number of similar species occur across Canada, among them the eastern trout lily (*Erythronium americanum*). White fawn lily is restricted to the extreme southwestern corner of British Columbia, where it favours the open woodlands of Vancouver Island and the Gulf Islands.

NOTES: The lily family is a large group of bulbed perennials characterized by parallel-veined leaves and flower parts occurring in threes.

Tall Oregon Grape

Berberis aquifolium
BERBERIDACEAE (BARBERRY FAMILY)

Shiny holly-like leaves and clusters of lemon-yellow flowers distinguish this evergreen shrub. Tall Oregon grape has five to seven leaflets per leaf, which after two or three years turn a brilliant orange red before dropping. The fragrant flowers bloom in early summer and mature into clusters of dark blue berries resembling bunches of grapes.

HABITAT/RANGE: Tall Oregon grape occurs throughout most of southern British Columbia, preferring sunny woodlands. A similar species, low Oregon grape (*Berberis nervosa*), is restricted to the southwestern part of the province, where it grows in shaded forests.

NOTES: Oregon grape berries were eaten by several Coast Indian groups and, although somewhat sour, are still enjoyed today as jelly or jam. Birds eat them only when other foods are scarce.

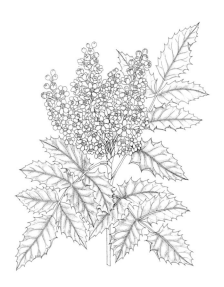

Bloodroot

Sanguinaria canadensis
PAPAVERACEAE (POPPY FAMILY)

The showy flowers of bloodroot bloom for only a short period each spring. The single bloom produced by each plant opens briefly in the warm spring sun to display between eight and twelve large white petals. The flower buds are enfolded and protected from the cold by deeply lobed leaves.

HABITAT/RANGE: Bloodroot thrives in rich moist woodlands from Manitoba to Quebec.

NOTES: The roots of this species contain a red sap that gives the plant its name. The red dye produced by the juice was valued both by Indians and by the early settlers.

Sea Blush

Plectritus congesta
VALERIANACEAE (VALERIAN
FAMILY)

Sea blush reaches the height of its blooming period in May, when meadows and rock ledges glow with its pastel hues. This diminutive annual bears a rounded cluster of pink (sometimes white) flowers so small that a hand lens is needed to discern them in detail. Opposite pairs of oblong leaves without stems grow from the angled, squarish stem.

HABITAT/RANGE: Restricted to the south coast of British Columbia, sea blush favours rocky knolls.

NOTES: Sea blush is often seen in bloom with a profusion of other spring wildflowers, particularly blue-eyed Mary and broad-leaved stonecrop.

Cream Violet

Viola striata
VIOLACEAE (VIOLET FAMILY)

This delicate violet unfolds its heart-shaped leaves in early spring. Each fragrant flower consists of five creamy petals, the lowest of which is marked by distinctive purple lines. These 'nectar lines' guide bees to the nectar sac located at the base of the lower petal. As they search for nectar the bees pollinate the flower they are visiting and receive a fresh dusting of pollen to fertilize the next violet they land upon.

HABITAT/RANGE: Many violet species are found across Canada. Cream violet thrives in moist open woodlands from southern Ontario to the Maritimes.

NOTES: The leaves and flowers of violets contain substantial amounts of vitamin C; both have been used in cough syrups to remedy colds. The edible flowers are often candied as decorations for cakes and other foods.

Scarlet Gilia

Gilia aggregata
POLEMONIACEAE (PHLOX FAMILY)

Although gilias may have yellow or white flowers, the scarlet form is the most common and spectacular. Opening in early summer, the trumpet-shaped blooms flare into five-pointed petals marked with white spots. In contrast to the resplendent flowers, the leaves are thin and drab.

HABITAT/RANGE: Scarlet gilia thrives in the open woods and on the dry slopes of western Canada, particularly in the southern interior of British Columbia.

NOTES: The generic name *Gilia* commemorates the eighteenth-century Spanish botanist Felipe Luis Gil; the specific name *aggregata*, meaning 'clustered', refers to the flowers.

Oval-leaved Blueberry

Vaccinium ovalifolium
ERICACEAE (HEATH FAMILY)

Oval-leaved blueberry, as its name implies, is distinguished from similar species by its leaves. This tall deciduous shrub produces its urn-shaped pinkish blossoms in early summer and is later festooned with dark blue berries. Usually covered with a pale bluish bloom, the berries are delicious either fresh or cooked.

HABITAT/RANGE: Oval-leaved blueberry thrives in cool, shady forests from sea level to subalpine heights. Like many other members of the heath family, it prefers acidic soils. At least eighteen *Vaccinium* species are found in all regions of Canada, including the arctic.

NOTES: The sweet, juicy fruit of oval-leaved blueberry is an important summer and early-fall food for grouse, songbirds, black bears, chipmunks, and deer mice.

Little Monkey Flower

Mimulus alsinoides

SCROPHULARIACEAE (FIGWORT FAMILY)

This diminutive annual pokes its bright yellow blooms only a few centimetres above the ground every spring. Each flower is marked by a number of reddish-purple spots on the lower lip, which may guide insects to the flower's reproductive organs. Partially hidden by the blooms are the small opposite leaves.

HABITAT/RANGE: Several monkey-flower species occur in woodlands across Canada, particularly in the west. Little monkey flower is restricted to the southern coast of British Columbia.

NOTES: Like some other members of the figwort family, the monkey flower has swollen corolla tubes that flare into two lips, with two lobes above and three below.

Canada Mayflower

Maianthemum canadense
LILIACEAE (LILY FAMILY)

This perennial brightens woodlands every spring with its shiny foliage and creamy white flowers. Spreading by underground stems, Canada mayflower often forms large colonies at the bases of mature trees. Generally only those plants with two or three leaves bear flowers; the others produce lush carpets of foliage. The delightfully fragrant flowers bloom throughout May, maturing into red berries by fall.

HABITAT/RANGE: Preferring deep, rich soils, Canada mayflower thrives in partially shaded woods across most of the country.

NOTES: The bright red berries of this plant have given rise to another common name: bead ruby. They are occasionally eaten by grouse, chipmunks, and deer mice.

Wild Columbine

Aquilegia canadensis
RANUNCULACEAE (BUTTERCUP FAMILY)

Wild columbine is a favourite among wild-flower enthusiasts. Its exquisitely shaped scarlet petals are often said to resemble five doves drinking at a dish. Each tubular red petal has a long, narrow spur at the back, which is brilliant yellow inside. After blooming the petals fall off, and as the fruit develops, the nodding flowers tilt to an upright position.

HABITAT/RANGE: Blooming from spring to early summer, wild columbine grows in rocky woodlands from Saskatchewan to Newfoundland. Several members of the *Aquilegia* genus are native to western Canada. Western columbine (*A. formosa*), which resembles wild columbine, blooms from the seashore to alpine areas.

NOTES: Hummingbirds attracted to the red blooms feed on the large amount of nectar contained in the flower spurs.

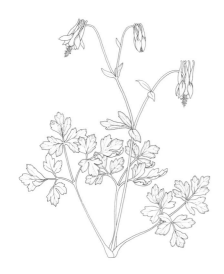

Common Blackberry

Rubus alleghieniensis
ROSACEAE (ROSE FAMILY)

Watch out for blackberry bushes: their sharp, sticky thorns are punishing guards for the delicious berries, which ripen in late summer after the white flowers have finished blooming. Some species bear male and female flowers on separate plants, with only the females producing fruit. Varying in height from a low shrub to a bush of over 2.5 metres, blackberry can form impenetrable thickets of thorns and foliage. The toothed leaflets generally occur in groups of three or five.

HABITAT/RANGE: Many blackberry species thrive in open woodlands and clearings across Canada. Common blackberry is found in open areas throughout southern Ontario, Quebec, and the Maritimes.

NOTES: Blackberries provide cover and reproductive sites for many birds and mammals. The fruit is an important food for songbirds, gamebirds, chipmunks, and squirrels.

Douglas Triteleia

Triteleia grandiflora
LILIACEAE (LILY FAMILY)

Once common, the trumpet-shaped flowers of Douglas triteleia are now a rare and delightful find. Look for the radiating cluster of five to twenty lavender-blue blossoms from spring to early summer. Several grass-like basal leaves and a long unbranched stem grow from the underground bulb.

HABITAT/RANGE: This species prefers open woods with deep rich soils. It is found in the dry extreme-southern interior of British Columbia, although even there it is becoming less and less common, and on Vancouver Island it is almost extinct.

NOTES: Many bulbs in the lily family are edible, and those of Douglas triteleia are considered choice. In the past they were steam-cooked and eaten by various Indian tribes.

Purple-flowering Raspberry

Rubus odoratus

ROSACEAE (ROSE FAMILY)

This fragrant shrub is most noticeable in summer, when it produces a succession of large magenta flowers. Almost as attractive as the blooms are the velvety-soft maple-shaped leaves, which grow alternately from thornless stems covered with sticky red hairs. Purple raspberry's acidic red fruit ripens by fall.

HABITAT/RANGE: Purple-flowering raspberry thrives in open woodlands from Ontario to Nova Scotia.

NOTES: The flowers of purple raspberry derive their fragrance from a coating of short hairs tipped with bead-like glands containing a sweet-scented gum.

Salal

Gaultheria shallon
ERICACEAE (HEATH FAMILY)

Distinguished by its thick evergreen leaves, salal is one of the most abundant shrubs of the Pacific rain forest. This ubiquitous plant varies in form from a creeping vine to an impenetrable wall of foliage twice the height of a man. The leathery leaves are collected and used commercially in flower arrangements. In early summer salal produces urn-shaped pinkish flowers borne in long one-sided clusters. They mature into mealy blue-black berries that ripen by late summer.

HABITAT/RANGE: Salal is common along the coast of British Columbia, with sporadic occurrences in wet forests in the province's interior. It thrives in moist acidic soils.

NOTES: In the past salal berries were the most plentiful and widely used fruit on the British Columbia coast. Several Indian groups ate them either fresh or dried into cakes resembling fruit leathers. They are still used to make a flavourful jam.

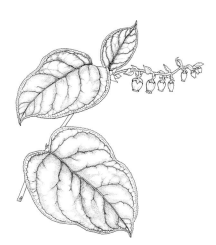

Broad-leaved Shooting Star

Dodecatheon hendersonii
PRIMULACEAE
(PRIMROSE FAMILY)

Clusters of these exquisitely shaped wild-flowers resemble cascades of shooting stars. Each blossom has reflexed magenta petals and a central beak-like stamen tube composed of coloured anthers joined around the style. This species is distinguished by its basal rosette of thick oval leaves.

HABITAT/RANGE: Several species of shooting star are found in moist open forests in the Yukon and the western provinces. Broad-leaved shooting star is restricted to the southern coast of British Columbia.

NOTES: The West Coast Indian languages have a number of lyrical names for this plant, including 'rain's navel' (Haida), 'curlew's bill' (Okanagan), and 'beautiful maiden' (Thompson). Its other common English name is 'peacock', presumably in reference to the shape of the flower.

Broad-leaved Stonecrop

Sedum spathulifolium
CRASSULACEAE
(STONECROP FAMILY)

A succulent plant, broad-leaved stonecrop is distinguished by its star-shaped yellow flowers and rosettes of fleshy leaves. As in a cactus, the flat, thumb-shaped leaves and thick stem store moisture to sustain the plant through periods of drought. In full sun the leaves may turn deep shades of pink.

HABITAT/RANGE: A number of *Sedum* species grow on rocks and cliffs across Canada. Broad-leaved stonecrop is common in southern British Columbia, growing in soil pockets on rocky and open hillsides.

NOTES: The fleshy young leaves of stonecrop are a favoured food of squirrels, pikas, and deer.

Wetland

With a salt-water shoreline that stretches for thousands of miles, from temperate to arctic regions; the largest bodies of fresh water in the world; and incalculable numbers of small lakes, marshes, potholes, and bogs, Canada is blessed with a great variety and abundance of wetlands. Although most flowering plants are terrestrial, many have adapted to living in or near water. Moisture-loving plants thrive in every type of condition, from freshwater marshes to still, cool acidic bogs, to flooded bottomlands. Their brilliant blooms and foliage enliven these biologically rich environments and provide invaluable food and shelter for wildlife.

The usually clear and regular pattern of vegetation around a marsh reflects each species' tolerance for water. The shoreline is rimmed with taller emergent plants such as bullrush, cat-tail, iris, and sweet flag, which show adaptations to their semi-aquatic existence. Air spaces in their underwater root-stocks facilitate gaseous exchange, and photosynthetic cells are concentrated in the above-water portions of stem and leaves. Further from shore is the zone of floating plants whose flat, broad leaves often cover the water in dense mats. Some, like yellow pond lily, are rooted. Buoyed up by air spaces, like sheets of cork-board, the broad lily pads have breathing mechanisms called stomata on their upper surfaces, and are not easily overturned; flexible stems allow them to rise and fall with changing water levels. Other species in this zone, like duckweed, are free-floating; because they can absorb

water and minerals so easily, their roots are very small. Furthest of all from shore are the submerged plants. These show the greatest departure from the structures of their terrestrial relatives. The stomata that might cause the plant to drown are usually lacking, and the conductive and stiffening tissues so critical to the success of land species are greatly reduced. Bladderwort has tiny bladders that not only trap small organisms but keep its flowering structures afloat, while milfoil and eel-grass have finely dissected or ribbon-like leaves that increase the surface area for absorption of dissolved gases and offer less resistance to currents.

Perhaps the most alluring of wetland habitats are the bogs. These highly acidic environments support a distinct community of plants, usually dominated by sphagnum moss. Although large portions of northern Canada are covered with spruce bogs, or muskeg, in the south the bogs are small and few in number. These remnants of northern habitat harbour many plants characteristic of the boreal forest zone, such as Labrador tea and small cranberry. One family, the carnivorous sundews, have adapted to the poor soil conditions by preying on insects for nitrogen.

Closely associated with wet habitats are plants that grow in the moist soils surrounding lakes, ponds, streams, and rivers. These species are able to survive flooding for at least part of the year. Western buttercup, skunk cabbage, marsh marigold, red-osier dogwood, and hardhack are among the plants one can expect to encounter around

most low-lying areas.

Few terrestrial habitats are capable of supporting the abundance of life found in a healthy marsh or pond. The liquid environment eliminates many of the problems — water and mineral transportation, moisture procurement, dessication, mechanical stresses from wind and weather — that land plants must overcome. Consequently, vegetative production is more efficient and capable of sustaining more wildlife. Although much of this harvest results from the growth of algae, many flowering plants also contribute greatly to the welfare of wildlife, particularly birds. Most of the continent's ducks, geese, and swans reproduce in or near the emergent vegetation of wetlands. Stands of cat-tail and bulrush provide nesting sites for herons, blackbirds, and marsh wrens, among many others. Muskrats as well as waterfowl feed on the leaves and stems, seeds or root-stocks of such species as duckweed, sago pondweed, widgeon grass, wild rice, smartweed, arrowhead, and sweet flag.

Marsh Ragwort

Senecio congestus

COMPOSITAE (COMPOSITE FAMILY)

This hardy perennial can be distinguished from similar species by its soft-haired stem, which is crowned by daisy-like yellow flower heads packed into dense woolly clusters. The numerous coarse, wavy-margined leaves are somewhat lobed and grow alternately up the tall stem.

HABITAT/RANGE: Marsh ragwort is common in streams, sloughs, and marshes, where it often forms a golden ring around the water's edge. Its range is circumpolar, extending through the Yukon, British Columbia, and the prairie provinces.

NOTES: Many *Senecio* species contain alkaloid compounds that are toxic to livestock. Tansy ragwort (*S. jacobaea*) is responsible for the death of considerable numbers of cattle and horses.

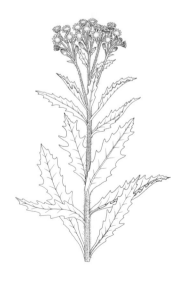

White Bog Orchid
Habenaria dilatata
ORCHIDACEAE (ORCHID FAMILY)

Often growing in large colonies, the tall flowering spikes of white bog orchid are a delectable find for insects. The numerous small white flowers are powerfully scented. Each waxy blossom has a distinctive hood and a lower lip that serves as a landing strip for insects. The lip widens at its base and extends backwards into a tail-like nectar spur under the flower. Narrow leaves clasping the slender stem are another distinguishing feature.

HABITAT/RANGE: White bog orchid is found in moist areas and bogs across most of Canada.

NOTES: The generic name *Habenaria*, meaning 'rein', refers to the long spur and lip that give this flower its other name: white rein orchid.

Swamp Laurel

Kalmia polifolia
ERICACEAE (HEATH FAMILY)

Swamp laurel is a dainty shrub distinguished by thin, twisting stems crowned by clusters of bright pink flowers. These star-shaped blossoms have an unusual mechanism: the anthers tucked into flaps on the tips of the petals are released when an insect touches the flower, dusting it with pollen. Growing in pairs, the leathery evergreen leaves are rolled slightly downwards at the edges and have fuzzy white undersurfaces.

HABITAT/RANGE: Distributed widely across most of Canada, swamp laurel is commonly found in bogs.

NOTES: The leaves and flowers of swamp laurel contain andromedotoxin, a compound poisonous to cattle and sheep.

Bittersweet Nightshade

Solanum dulcamara
SOLANACEAE (NIGHTSHADE FAMILY)

A perennial vine that blooms throughout the summer, bittersweet nightshade bears small clusters of flowers shaped like shooting stars. The reflexed violet petals surround a protruding beak formed by the yellow stamens. Often found on the same vine as the flowers, the attractive berries change colour from green to bright scarlet as they ripen.

HABITAT/RANGE: Bittersweet nightshade is a Eurasian immigrant that ranges across Canada, preferring wet roadsides and marshy shores.

NOTES: The foliage of plants in the nightshade family contains a highly toxic alkaloid known to cause sickness and death in animals and humans. The fruits of some species, including this nightshade, are occasionally eaten by birds like the common song sparrow.

Closely related to tomatoes, nightshade berries are ▷ eaten by many kinds of wildlife.

Hardhack

Spiraea douglasii
ROSACEAE (ROSE FAMILY)

Hardhack is one of the most common shrubs of moist open areas, easily recognized by its steeple-like clusters of tiny pink flowers and its oblong leaves. Growing alternately up the slender reddish-brown stems, the leaves are distinctly coarse-toothed at the tip and coated underneath with grey hairs. After blooming all summer, the flowers dry into brown husks that remain on the bush long after the foliage has dropped, making hardhack conspicuous even during the winter.

HABITAT/RANGE: *Spiraea douglasii* is restricted to southern British Columbia. A similar species, *S. tomentosa*, occurs east of Manitoba.

NOTES: Members of the *Spiraea* genus are unique in the Rose family in that their leaves lack stipules.

Red Elderberry

Sambucus racemosa
CAPRIFOLIACEAE (HONEYSUCKLE FAMILY)

Another common wetland shrub, red elderberry is distinguished by its long clusters of fragrant creamy-white blossoms and five to seven large toothed leaflets. The small saucer-shaped flowers bloom throughout the spring and early summer, exuding a heavy but pleasant scent that attracts a number of insects. After flowering this tall bushy shrub will be aflame with bunches of bright red berries.

HABITAT/RANGE: Red elderberry is found in moist soils throughout the western provinces. Similar species occur across most of Canada, except in arid regions.

NOTES: Red elderberry fruits are sought after by a variety of birds, particularly the band-tailed pigeon.

Round-leaved Sundew

Drosera rotundifolia
DROSERACEAE (SUNDEW FAMILY)

It is the extraordinary foliage, not the inconspicuous white flowers, that attract attention to this carnivorous plant. The round green leaves bristle with small red hairs tipped with sticky beads. Glands inside each of these minute globes exude a clear, sticky liquid. Any insect attracted to the red tentacles is trapped at once by the viscous hairs, which slowly close around it. Once the insect's juices are digested, the leaves uncurl and the remains of the skeleton are scattered by the wind.

HABITAT/RANGE: This is one of five sundew species found in bogs and swamps across Canada.

NOTES: Sundews prey on insects to obtain nutrients, such as nitrogen and phosphorus, that they cannot secure from wet peat bogs.

Yellow Iris

Iris pseudacorus
IRIDIACEAE (IRIS FAMILY)

The regal blooms of yellow iris grace wetlands in early summer. This showy perennial grows in patches, spreading by underground rhizomes. The flower is composed of three large sepals (often mistaken for petals) and three small upright petals rising above the curved and modified stigmas. Once the flower is pollinated the petals quickly shrivel and the portion below develops into a fruit capsule containing the seeds.

HABITAT/RANGE: Introduced from Europe, yellow iris is found in wet ditches and along lakeshores and swamps across most of southern Canada.

NOTES: Iris leaves and roots are poisonous to humans but valuable to wildlife. Waterfowl often seek cover in the dense clumps of stiff, sword-like foliage, and muskrats feed on the underwater roots.

Pussy Willow

Salix discolor
SALICACEAE (WILLOW FAMILY)

With more than seventy-five closely related willow species in Canada, identification is often difficult. Pussy willow has the characteristic willow leaf: long and smooth, with slightly toothed edges. This shrub is most noticeable in spring, when its fluffy white catkins are in flower. Male and female flowers grow on different shrubs.

HABITAT/RANGE: Most willows thrive in the moist, fertile soil of bottomlands, river banks, and lake margins. Pussy willow ranges from Newfoundland west to Alberta, usually growing in clumps.

NOTES: Willows are an important food source for wildlife. The buds and tender twigs are staples for grouse and ptarmigan, while the twigs, leaves, and bark feed rabbits and hoofed browsers like elk, moose, and deer.

◁ Tree swallows frequent willows in search of the insects attracted to their spring blossoms. The branches often serve as courtship perches.

Cow Parsnip

Heracleum lanatum
UMBELLIFERAE (PARSLEY FAMILY)

This hardy perennial towers over most other wetland and roadside plants. Its flat-topped flower cluster, made up of numerous small white flowers with notched petals, grows to a massive size, sometimes measuring more than 20 centimetres across. The large leaves, divided into maple-like segments, emerge from a clasping sheath that branches off from the woolly main stem.

HABITAT/RANGE: Cow parsnip thrives in moist soils across Canada.

NOTES: The leaves of cow parsnip are foraged by domestic and wild animals, including bear, elk, and mountain sheep.

Small Cranberry

Vaccinium oxycoccos
ERICACEAE (HEATH FAMILY)

A slender evergreen vine, small cranberry is not always easy to see. The tiny pink flowers, which resemble miniature shooting stars, bloom in summer. The leathery alternate leaves are deep green above and grey-white below. By fall the vine is festooned with little red berries.

HABITAT/RANGE: Common in bogs across most of Canada, small cranberry thrives in moss and peat.

NOTES: Cranberries were sought after by the pioneers, who called them 'crane berries' because of the flower's resemblance to the head and neck of a crane.

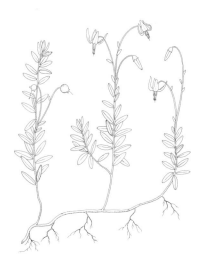

Broad-leaved Cat-Tail

Typha latifolia
TYPHACEAE (CAT-TAIL FAMILY)

The cat-tail is one of our most familiar wetland plants. The velvety brown 'tail' is actually a spike of female flowers. When in bloom they are green, but after pollination they turn brown and develop seeds. Located above the tail is the male portion of the flower; it is covered with short floppy stamens that shed pollen into the air.

HABITAT/RANGE: Cat-tails are found along the edges of swamps and ponds across Canada.

NOTES: Cat-tail marshes are extremely productive for wildlife. Muskrats, for instance, not only eat the root-stalks but use the leaves to build their lodges.

◁ A cat-tail provides nest-building material for a marsh wren.

71

Water Smartweed

Polygonum amphibium
POLYGONACEAE (BUCKWHEAT FAMILY)

Water smartweed is an amphibious plant, able to survive both in and out of the water. It is commonly found around the water's edge where, spreading by underwater roots, it often forms large colonies. The broad leaves lie flat on the water, but on land they are narrower and grow alternately up the smooth stem. The vibrant pink flowers have five sepals rather than petals. In any cluster only a few bloom at any one time; each quickly ripens to a single black seed.

HABITAT/RANGE: Water smartweed can be found along the shallow shores of lakes and ponds across Canada.

NOTES: The seeds of this species constitute about one-quarter of the diet of some of our most common songbirds and waterfowl, including fox and song sparrows, cardinals, mallards, pintails, blue- and green-winged teal, and Canada geese.

Sweet Flag

Acorus calamus
ARACEAE (ARUM FAMILY)

Sweet flag is easily recognized by the large flowering spadix that juts out at an angle from the succulent main stem. The minute densely packed flowers are greenish-yellow and bloom in early summer. Growing in clumps, sweet flag's rigid, sword-like leave resemble those of wild irises.

HABITAT/RANGE: Sweet flag thrives in we meadows and along pond edges and shores across most of central and eastern Canada

NOTES: After prolonged boiling the roots o sweet flag may be candied to produce a confection with a strong gingery flavour.

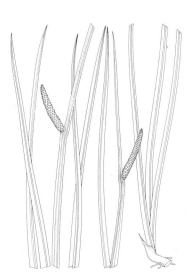

Marsh Marigold

Caltha palustris
RANUNCULACEAE (BUTTERCUP
FAMILY)

The showy flowers of marsh marigold mark it as a member of the buttercup family. Blooming throughout the spring, the flowers usually occur in pairs and are made up not of true petals but of sepals. When not in flower, marsh marigold can be recognized by its large kidney-like leaves, which are characteristically folded.

HABITAT/RANGE: Marsh marigold is found across most of Canada in shallow waters, along shorelines, and in moist to wet woods.

NOTES: The bright yellow flowers of this plant produce a soft golden dye.

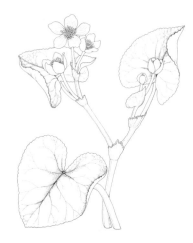

White Water-Lily

Nymphaea odorata
NYMPHAEACEAE (WATER-LILY FAMILY)

Fragrant white water-lilies adorn lakeshores and ponds with their elegant blossoms. Layers of tapered white petals surround the brilliant yellow stamens at the centre of the flower. Almost as decorative as the bloom are the lily's large platter-like pads, which often form dense mats. Unlike the leaves of terrestrial plants, which have stomata (breathing structures) on their undersides, water-lily leaves contain these pores on the upper surfaces, so that they will be exposed to the air.

HABITAT/RANGE: White water-lily is found across most of Canada in shallow lakes and ponds.

NOTES: The seeds of white water-lily are eaten by various ducks. Moose browse on the foliage, stems, and roots.

Red-Osier Dogwood

Cornus stolonifera
CORNACEAE (DOGWOOD FAMILY)

Red-osier dogwood is most noticeable in the fall, when its leaves and bark glow a fiery crimson. Like other dogwoods, it has deeply veined leaves and florets with four petals, four sepals, and four stamens. The flat-topped clusters of greenish-white flowers bloom in early summer and mature into white berries by late summer.

HABITAT/RANGE: Often forming impenetrable thickets, red-osier dogwood ranges across Canada. It prefers the moist soils in open woods or along streams and roadsides.

NOTES: The fleshy fruits of dogwood are very valuable to wildlife, particularly birds. Cardinals, evening grosbeaks, band-tailed pigeons, robins, and wood ducks are especially fond of the berries, which constitute about one-quarter of their diet.

Beavers feed on the tender bark of red-osier dogwood. ▷

Skunk Cabbage

Lysichitum americanum
ARACEAE (ARUM FAMILY)

Skunk cabbage is most noticeable in early spring, when it begins to flower. The flowers are tightly clustered on a club-like spadix wrapped in a golden leafy covering. When this spathe begins to fade, the enormous waxy oval leaves appear. Probably the largest of any native plant in British Columbia, these often measure more than half a metre across and more than a metre long.

HABITAT/RANGE: Skunk cabbage grows in river forests and swamps in British Columbia. A different, smaller skunk cabbage occurs in eastern Canada from Nova Scotia to eastern Manitoba.

NOTES: Despite the pungent odour of skunk cabbage, deer and bears browse on its leaves. Waterfowl and upland gamebirds occasionally eat the large seeds.

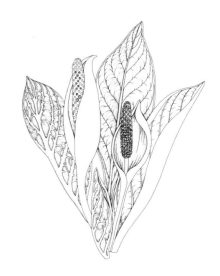

Purple Loosestrife

Lythrum salicaria
LYTHRACEAE (LOOSESTRIFE FAMILY)

Supported on swaying stalks almost as tall as a man, these foot-long flower spikes blaze magenta throughout the summer. The bright hue of the small six-petalled flowers attracts a wide variety of insects, particularly bees and butterflies, which feed on the nectar. Clasping the slender stem below the flower stalk are the lance-shaped leaves. Although these usually occur in pairs, they may also grow in whorls of three or more around the stalk.

HABITAT/RANGE: Introduced from Europe in the early 1800s, purple loosestrife is now common in meadows and marshes across Canada.

NOTES: The rapid spread of purple loosestrife has given rise to concern. It is estimated that one healthy plant can produce up to 90,000 seeds, enabling it to crowd out many native species. Unlike some of the native plants it replaces, purple loosestrife has little food value for wildlife.

Labrador Tea

Ledum groenlandicum
ERICACEAE (HEATH FAMILY)

Labrador tea is a scraggly evergreen shrub easily identified by its narrow leathery leaves. Growing alternately on the twisted stems, they have strongly rolled edges and a fuzzy undersurface of white hairs that become rusty with age. Clusters of white flowers begin blooming in May and continue throughout the summer. Each flower is made up of five small petals with five to eight protruding stamens.

HABITAT/RANGE: This is a typical shrub of peat bogs, muskegs, and wet mountain meadows. It usually grows in association with sphagnum moss and is found throughout most of Canada, including the arctic.

NOTES: Indians and early explorers made a tea from the aromatic leaves of Labrador tea. When crushed the foliage exudes an unusual rosemary-cedar scent.

Yellow Pond Lily

Nuphar polysepalum
NYMPHAEACEAE (WATER-LILY
FAMILY)

Lush mats of floating foliage attract the eye to this native water-lily. Rising above the heart-shaped pads, the showy flower has conspicuous yellow sepals that are often mistaken for petals. At the centre of the flower is a toadstool-shaped stigma surrounded by purplish stamens. Often the flying insects that pollinate the flower take a rest on the lily's broad pads.

HABITAT/RANGE: Yellow pond-lily brightens lakes, ponds, and streams across Canada.

NOTES: The underwater leaves of yellow pond-lily are a year-round food source for beaver and muskrat.

Prairie and Meadow

Prairie landscapes occur in areas where the rainfall is too limited to support the growth of trees. Although a few patches remain in southwestern Ontario, by far the greatest expanses of prairie in Canada are within the borders of the four western provinces. Here we find many species adapted to life in a dry, wind-buffeted environment. These arid conditions are most extreme in some regions of the southern prairie provinces and the interior river valleys of British Columbia, where sparse rainfall and hot summers create habitats dominated by semi-desert plants. But other vast tracts of the Canadian landscape are also devoid of trees. Although they receive ample rain, forest growth is prevented by the work of the bulldozer, the plough, and the chainsaw. The plant communities of these disturbed areas—meadows, roadsides, ditches, vacant lots, logging clear-cuts—are characterized by species, many of European origin, that are able to establish themselves quickly on ground where the natural vegetation has been removed.

Many prairie plants show obvious adaptations to their dry, open environment. Grasses, the most abundant flowering plants of the prairies, have blossoms that are small and inconspicuous, since for pollination they rely not on insects but on the almost constant winds. Other species produce seeds specially designed for wind dispersal. The silky seed filaments of cat's ear are like parachutes, carrying the seeds great distances. The main stem of tumbleweed weakens and breaks off near the ground; driven by the wind, the spherical shrub then rolls across the prairie, shedding seeds as it goes. Other plants have evolved in such a way as to limit the stress of too much wind and too little water. The low-lying prairie crocus, for instance, finds shelter among taller grasses. Many prairie plants have two root systems: extensive surface roots that spread over large areas to absorb rainfall before it evaporates, as well as tap roots up to 3 metres long, to reach the more dependable water reserves deep underground.

Canada's driest regions support a desert-like flora dominated by sage brush, antelope bush, and even cacti. Prickly pear and pincushion cacti have thick-skinned succulent stems that store water to sustain the plants through long periods of drought; also functioning as leaves, they are covered with needle-sharp spines that guard the valuable water stores from grazing animals. The leaves of sage and scarlet mallow are insulated with hairs to reduce evaporation from heat and wind. The roots of many species have become toughened, to penetrate the hard, sun-baked soils and rocky ground.

The invasion of many areas by human industry and agriculture has created open habitats favouring species able to germinate and propagate quickly. One of the most common plants in these disturbed areas is the thistle, which spreads quickly from fast-growing root-stocks that run under the surface and send up new shoots. To ensure insect pollination and seed production, the flowers of many plants are bright-coloured and sweet-scented. Species like sunflowers and gaillardia, which have composite flower heads producing hundreds of seeds each season, are common. Introduced species are particularly successful. Brought from Europe, in North America they encounter few of the insects, mammals, or plants that formerly limited their growth. Not having to contend with many of the agents of control that work in a balanced ecosystem, many have displaced the native species that would normally recolonize these habitats.

Canada's wild prairies, fields, and so-called waste areas are among our most vital wildlife habitats. Providing food for deer and antelope, the brushy cover also serves as nesting habitat for pheasant, grouse, quail, and even waterfowl, along with countless numbers of mice, voles, rabbits, hares, and ground squirrels. In turn these herbivores attract birds of prey, foxes, coyotes, bobcats, badgers, rattlesnakes, and other carnivores. Our fencerows, roadsides, and meadows also harbour a varied insect community, including valuable seed populations of predatory insects; increasing in numbers at the appropriate moment, these help to limit periodic outbreaks of agricultural insect pests.

Blue Iris

Iris versicolor
IRIDACEAE (IRIS FAMILY)

Like prisms refracting light, blue iris flowers present a rainbow of subtly blended colours. The large down-curved sepals (often mistaken for petals) are prominently veined with yellow and white. Almost as distinctive as the blooms are the tall flower stalks and the sword-like leaves, which grow directly from the rhizome.

HABITAT/RANGE: *Iris versicolor* is common in moist fields and meadows from southern Manitoba east.

NOTES: Numerous bees follow the guide lines on the sepals to the nectar reservoir located in the thickened green base of the flower. In the process, pollen is scraped off the bee's back by the modified pistils, and the anthers dust the visitor with a fresh batch for transport to the next bloom.

Black-eyed Susan

Rudbeckia serotina
COMPOSITAE (COMPOSITE FAMILY)

The brilliant orange ray florets of black-eyed Susan attract a variety of insects to the dark purple disk florets at the centre of the flower head. Notice that in the photograph the outermost rings of disk florets are dusted with ripe yellow pollen; this means that the florets are in the male stage of the flowering sequence. Once the pollen is dispersed the pistils will open to receive pollen from other plants. The rest of the disk florets open in concentric rings towards the centre of the flower head.

HABITAT/RANGE: Originally a mid-western plant, several species of black-eyed Susan now thrive across Canada in dry meadows and disturbed areas.

NOTES: The rough, bristly stems and hairy leaves of this plant reduce evaporation, enabling it to survive arid conditions.

Prickly Pear Cactus

Opuntia fragilis
CACTACEAE (CACTUS FAMILY)

The waxy yellow blossoms of prickly pear cactus illuminate the desert each summer. Like other cacti, this leafless perennial has thick succulent stems that not only serve to store moisture but also function as leaves, carrying out photosynthesis and transpiration. Prickly pear hugs the parched soil in large, spreading mats.

HABITAT/RANGE: Common in the desert and prairie regions of western Canada, this species thrives on dry sandy hillsides. It is one of the few cacti in Canada.

NOTES: The numerous thorns of cacti do not deter antelope, deer, and big-horn sheep, which eat both the sweet fruits and the spongy stems without apparent injury.

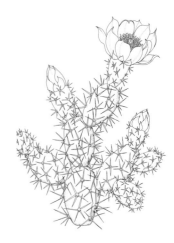

Bitter Root

Lewisia rediviva
PORTULACACEAE (PURSLANE FAMILY)

Spectacular rose, pink, or white blossoms adorn this low-lying semi-desert plant in late May or June. Each large bloom displays between twelve and eighteen waxen petals that unfurl only in bright sunlight. A rosette of narrow succulent leaves stores water to sustain bitter root during periods of drought.

HABITAT/RANGE: Bitter root is restricted to arid open areas in British Columbia. It is commonly found with sagebrush and near ponderosa-pine woods.

NOTES: This species was an important food source for the Plains Indians, who ate the white interior pulp of the roots. Later named bitter root by settlers, it was collected by Meriwether Lewis of the famous Lewis and Clark botanical expedition, after whom the genus was named.

Devil's Paintbrush

Hieracium aurantiacum

COMPOSITAE (COMPOSITE FAMILY)

The fiery crimson flower heads of devil's paintbrush open and close each day in response to light intensity. Also known as hawkweeds, these hardy perennials grow in colonies, like dandelions, and are among the most conspicuous blooms to cover open areas in early summer. The spreading basal rosette of hairy leaves keeps competition down by preventing other plants from becoming established.

HABITAT/RANGE: Both introduced and native hawkweeds thrive in fields and woodlands across Canada. Devil's paintbrush, an introduced species, is most common in dry meadows in the east.

NOTES: According to legend, hawks used these plants to sharpen their vision. It was mistakenly assumed that the hawks were eating the plants, but in fact they were hunting mice and voles in the fields where hawkweeds grow.

Alsike Clover

Trifolium hybridum
LEGUMINOSAE (PEA FAMILY)

The fragrant flowers of this species tint fields a pinkish hue throughout the summer. As in other clovers, the flower head is composed of many tiny flowers grouped together. Because only a few flowers bloom at a time, the period in which pollination is possible is extended. After the flowers are pollinated their petals droop and turn brown (as in the photograph) before falling off.

HABITAT/RANGE: An introduced perennial, Alsike clover thrives in fields and meadows throughout eastern and central Canada.

NOTES: As the generic name *Trifolium* implies, clovers usually have three leaflets, though the odd lucky one may have four. Their foliage is relished by a number of small mammals and birds.

Clover is one of the giant swallowtail butterfly's ▷ favoured sources of nectar.

Prairie Sunflower

Helianthus petiolaris
COMPOSITAE (COMPOSITE FAMILY)

Daisy-like yellow flower heads of prairie sunflower smile into the open prairie skies. Growing from an underground rhizome, this robust perennial produces rough, wedge-shaped alternate leaves on tall hairy stems. Wild sunflowers are among the first plants to become established in abandoned fields, releasing toxins to inhibit the spread of other plants around them.

HABITAT/RANGE: There are at least sixty sunflower species native to North America, particularly the prairies. Prairie sunflower thrives in sandy soils along roadsides and in dry open areas.

NOTES: Long before the first settlers arrived in North America, sunflowers were grown by the Plains Indians for the oil and flour they could obtain from the seeds. Today the larger seeds of the cultivated sunflower are still an important oil crop. Many birds, as well as chipmunks and squirrels, also relish sunflower seeds.

Cushion Cactus

Coryphantha vivipara
CACTACEAE (CACTUS FAMILY)

Like other members of the large cactus family, this tufted perennial has small pin-cushion-like stems covered with spines that are modified leaves. In the absence of normal leaves, the green succulent stems take over the normal photosynthetic function. Cushion cactus blooms in July, producing large, showy magenta blossoms with many sepals, petals, and stamens, and one pistil. After pollination the flowers mature into fleshy green berries, which turn brown on ripening.

HABITAT/RANGE: Cushion cactus is common on dry open prairies, particularly in southern Alberta.

NOTES: In this photograph the bee's pollen baskets, located on its hind legs, are filled with ripe yellow dust for easy transport back to the hive.

Bull Thistle

Cirsium vulgare
COMPOSITAE (COMPOSITE FAMILY)

To prevent trampling and grazing by larger animals, thistles are guarded with sharp spines on their leaves, flowers, and, in some cases, stems. One of the most vigorous and well-armed species, bull thistle has prickles not only on its stem but also on the upper surface of its leaves and along the leaf edges. Each of the bracts beneath the large purplish flower head also ends in a sharp spine.

HABITAT/RANGE: A wide variety of native and introduced thistles thrive in fields and waste places across Canada.

NOTES: Butterflies are often seen feeding on thistle flowers, and the painted lady (*Cynthis cardui*) lays its eggs on the leaves. Gold-finches use the silky seed filaments to build their nests.

Wild Gaillardia

Gaillardia aristata
COMPOSITAE (COMPOSITE FAMILY)

A common sight on the open prairie, wild gaillardia blooms throughout July and August. It is easily recognized by the numerous tawny-orange cleft rays surrounding the purplish-brown disk florets at the centre of the flower head. Growing from a slender tap-root, this tall, showy perennial has an abundance of hairy, greyish-green alternate leaves that become smaller towards the top of the stem.

HABITAT/RANGE: Wild gaillardia is found in dry soils along roadsides and on the open prairie.

NOTES: Like many plants that grow in open areas, wild gaillardia produces an abundance of seeds that are dispersed by the strong prairie winds.

Field Mustard

Brassica campestris
CRUCIFERAE (MUSTARD FAMILY)

Fields washed with the bright yellow of blooming mustard are a familiar early-summer sight across the country. Growing in clusters, the small yellow flowers of field mustard have the typical cross shape of their family. Each flower is perfectly symmetrical, displaying four sepals, four petals, six stamens, and a pistil. After flowering, field mustard can be recognized by its narrow, elongated fruit capsule and smooth leaves that clasp the stem.

HABITAT/RANGE: This introduced plant thrives in fields and waste places across Canada.

NOTES: Mustard seeds are relished by game- and songbirds, particularly the common house finch.

Ox-eye Daisy

Chrysanthemum leucanthemum
COMPOSITAE (COMPOSITE FAMILY)

Clustered together on a daisy flower head are many tiny yellow disk florets surrounded by white petal-like ray florets. All the disk florets have both female and male parts, which bloom in sequence to ensure cross-pollination. They open in concentric rings towards the centre of the flower head, beginning with the male stage and ending with the female. When a bee visits a daisy, it alights at the outermost edge of the yellow disk and pollinates the elongated pistils with the pollen from the last flower it visited. As it feeds, the bee crawls towards the centre of the disk, where it is dusted with pollen from florets in the male stage.

HABITAT/RANGE: An introduced species, ox-eye daisy is now widespread in fields and meadows across Canada. This hardy perennial is tolerant of a variety of soil conditions, as well as drought and frost.

NOTES: Bees and butterflies feed on the nectar and pollen produced by daisies. The grasshopper in the photograph may be just resting before buzzing off to feed on foliage and grasses.

Prairie Crocus

Anemone patens
RANUNCULACEAE (BUTTERCUP
FAMILY)

The silky, lavender-blue blooms of prairie crocus herald the end of the gruelling prairie winter. Borne on a hairy stem, the solitary flower consists of five to seven petal-like sepals and numerous stamens and pistils. In early summer the sepals fall away and the flower matures into a fluffy seed head. At this stage prairie crocus can be recognized by its woolly, deeply cut leaves and elongated flowering stalk.

HABITAT/RANGE: One of the most conspicuous of anemone species on the prairie, this low-lying perennial thrives in dry grasslands and on open slopes from southeastern British Columbia to Manitoba.

NOTES: Prairie crocus is also commonly called pasque flower, because it blooms around Easter. Early European settlers used the purple sepals to dye Easter eggs.

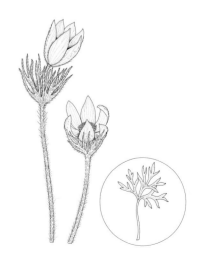

Birdsfoot Trefoil

Lotus corniculatus
LEGUMINOSAE (PEA FAMILY)

Birdsfoot trefoil bears small rounded clusters of pea-like flowers in early summer. These waxy blooms mature into narrow, pointed seed pods that some people have found reminiscent of a bird's foot. Others suggest that the common name refers instead to the foliage made up of three leaflets — the trefoil. Two stipules grow at the base of the petiole.

HABITAT/RANGE: Birdsfoot trefoil is commonly found in fields and along roadsides. Apparently introduced on both the Atlantic and Pacific coasts, it is gradually moving into central Canada.

NOTES: Birdsfoot trefoil is a European pasture plant often used as a forage crop for cattle.

Viper's Bugloss

Echium vulgare
BORAGINACEAE (BORAGE FAMILY)

An interesting time to observe the bright blue flowers of viper's bugloss is in mid-afternoon, when nectar production reaches a peak and the plants are swarming with bees. Like other members of the borage family, viper's bugloss bears a five-petalled tubular flower with five protruding stamens. Growing in dense clusters, the flowers open one at a time from a purplish-red bud. The hairy silvery-green leaves grow alternately from the tall bristly stem.

HABITAT/RANGE: Introduced from Europe, viper's bugloss is now widely distributed in fields across Canada, particularly in Ontario and Quebec.

NOTES: Viper's bugloss was brought to North America because of its reputed value in herbal remedies, especially as a cure for snake bite.

Moss Phlox

Phlox hoodii
POLEMONIACEAE (PHLOX FAMILY)

A low-tufted perennial, moss phlox spreads its woody stems and spiny leaves over the dry prairie. In early spring masses of flowers punctuate its otherwise drab appearance. Usually white, the small, inconspicuous blooms may occasionally be pale blue or purple. Each flower has a wheel-shaped corolla consisting of five petals, a form typical of all phloxes.

HABITAT/RANGE: Moss phlox is common in the prairie provinces, particularly in southern Alberta. After flowering, the mat-forming foliage constitutes a large portion of the ground cover on eroded hillsides with shallow soils.

NOTES: The cobwebby hairs covering its densely tufted foliage enable moss phlox to conserve water by reducing the evaporation caused by the constant winds of the dry open prairie.

Common Dandelion

Taraxacum officinale
COMPOSITAE (COMPOSITE FAMILY)

The familiar dandelion is one of our most successful wildflowers. Its year-round rosette of leaves spreads out to keep other plants away, and its long tap-root is virtually indestructible unless totally removed from the soil. In addition, dandelion's numerous plume-borne seeds are dispersed by the slightest breeze. Interestingly, dandelion seeds are not produced through pollination but grow directly from the ovules. Thus a flower head will still produce seeds even if it does not open.

HABITAT/RANGE: Common dandelion is abundant in fields and meadows and along roadsides across Canada.

NOTES: Dandelion leaves are delicious either steamed or fresh in salads. The seeds are frequently eaten by songbirds, chipmunks, and pocket gophers.

◁ A honey bee dusted with pollen feeds on a dandelion head.

Milfoil

Achillea millefolium

COMPOSITAE (COMPOSITE FAMILY)

Milfoil, or yarrow, is one of Canada's most familiar field flowers, blooming throughout the summer. Each of the clustered blooms is like a miniature daisy made up of yellow disk and white ray florets. The perfectly camouflaged crab spider in this photograph is waiting to ambush one of the many insects that feed on milfoil's nectar and pollen.

HABITAT/RANGE: Milfoil is extremely adaptable and can survive practically any elevation or soil condition. In addition to the native forms, there is an introduced yarrow, from Europe, which is common in fields and along roadsides across Canada.

NOTES: The specific name *millefolium*, 'thousand-leaved', refers to milfoil's finely divided foliage. These aromatic leaves were used for centuries to stop bleeding and relieve stomach ailments.

Self-heal

Prunella vulgaris
LABIATAE (MINT FAMILY)

Self-heal's most recognizable feature is its spike of violet-blue flowers, which bloom from early summer to fall. The tiny, two-lipped tubular flowers are characteristic of plants in the mint family. Notice that the three-lobed lower lip is distinctively fringed and tufted with white hairs. After flowering, the spike elongates and the purple-green bracts persist as brown scales. The lance-shaped leaves of this low-lying perennial grow opposite one another up the square stem.

HABITAT/RANGE: This introduced species thrives in moist fields and meadows across most of Canada.

NOTES: As its common name implies, self-heal has been used through the centuries as a remedy for various ailments, including sore throats, internal bleeding, and external wounds.

Butter-and-Eggs

Linaria vulgaris
SCROPHULARIACEAE (FIGWORT FAMILY)

Easily distinguished by its long stalk of yellow and orange speckled flowers and its blue-green leaves, butter-and-eggs is one of our most common field flowers. Bumble-bees are attracted to its bright orange landing platform and use their long tongue to reach into the nectar spur at the base of the flower. If you hold a flower up to the light, you can see how much nectar is in the spur. Flowers with less nectar have recently been fed on by insects.

HABITAT/RANGE: An introduced perennial, butter-and-eggs spreads in colonies along roadsides and in dry fields across Canada.

NOTES: The generic name *Linaria* refers to the similarity of the thin, linear leaves to those of flax (*linum*) and also gives the plant its other common name: toadflax.

Scarlet Mallow

Sphaeralcea coccinea
MALVACEAE (MALLOW FAMILY)

In early summer the globe-shaped blooms of scarlet mallow set the dry prairie aflame. Borne on a short leaf spike, the crêpe-papery flower consists of five petals, five sepals, and numerous stamens joined together around the pistil. As in many other prairie flowers, the stems and divided leaves are covered with soft woolly hairs that reduce water evaporation.

HABITAT/RANGE: Scarlet mallow grows in sprawling mats in sandy soils on the prairies and grasslands of western Canada.

NOTES: Although plants in the mallow family are found across Canada, the scarlet species is one of the few natives.

White Campion

Lychnis alba
CARYOPHYLLACEAE (PINK FAMILY)

White campion's sweet fragrance attracts insects as well as flower enthusiasts. The inflated sac beneath the petals is actually formed by the sepals of the flower joined together. On any one plant there are only male or female flowers. The females mature into fruit capsules containing 350 to 500 seeds each. An average plant will produce about sixty capsules, totalling 24,000 seeds per year. Although this seems an astonishingly large number, only a few will germinate and reach maturity; the rest remain dormant or are eaten by insects and birds.

HABITAT/RANGE: An introduced species, white campion is common in fields and waste places across Canada.

NOTES: The blooms of white campion open after dark, attracting night-flying insects. Long-tubed mouths enable these insects to reach deep into the floral tubes to suck out the nectar.

Cat's Ear

Hypochoeris radicata
COMPOSITAE (COMPOSITE FAMILY)

Sometimes mistaken for a dandelion because of its similar yellow flower head, cat's ear can be recognized by its large basal leaves, which are distinctly hairy on both sides. It also has small bracts scattered up and down its otherwise smooth stem. As in other members of the composite family, the flower head is composed of many individual flowers grouped together. Unlike daisies, however, which have both ray and disk florets, cat's ear has only rays, containing both male and female parts. After blooming all summer, the flowers mature and the seeds are dispersed by the wind.

HABITAT/RANGE: This introduced perennial is common across most of Canada.

NOTES: Cat's ear is one of many plants introduced to Canada from Eurasia. Although these exotics have added to our floral diversity, some—including this species—are particularly invasive and have crowded out many native plants.

Canada Goldenrod

Solidago canadensis
COMPOSITAE (COMPOSITE FAMILY)

Although the brilliant yellow, plume-like flower clusters of goldenrod are generally of little interest to humans, their scent and colour attract a variety of insect pollinators. The sticky nectar and pollen produced by hundreds of tiny flowers adhere to insects like the bee in this photograph. Treehoppers and goldenrod beetles eat the saw-edged leaves, which grow alternately up the tall stems. A variety of carnivorous spiders and ambush bugs prey on these insects.

HABITAT/RANGE: More than a hundred goldenrod species occupy a wide variety of habitats throughout North America. One of the most common native goldenrods, this one is found in dry fields and meadows.

NOTES: With so many closely related species, hybridization (in which pollen from one species fertilizes the female parts of another) is common.

Purple Snakeroot

Sanicula bipinnatifida
UMBELLIFERAE (PARSLEY FAMILY)

Flowering in early summer, the unusual blooms of purple snakeroot call for a closer look. The whole flower is a reddish-purple hue, from the in-curved petals to the stamens and pistil. Like many plants in the parsley family, snakeroot is pollinated by insects that feed on the nectar produced by the closely packed florets making up the flower head. The leaves of this species are distinguished by the lacerate-edged leaves.

HABITAT/RANGE: Found on open slopes, purple snakeroot is restricted to the southwestern coast of British Columbia and Vancouver Island. A number of snakeroot species range across western Canada.

NOTES: The generic name *Sanicula* is derived from the Latin *sanare*, 'to heal'. The Plains Indians used several species of this plant as a remedy for snake bites.

Blue-eyed Grass

Sisyrinchium angustifolium
IRIDACEAE (IRIS FAMILY)

The small, delicate flowers of blue-eyed grass last only a day before withering under the summer sun. The end of each of the six petals is distinctly marked by a fine tip. Insects are guided by nectar lines on the purple petals to the brilliant yellow column at the centre of the flower, formed by the filaments joined in a tube around the style. In fact not a grass at all, this species has the flattened, sword-like leaves typical of the iris family.

HABITAT/RANGE: Several species of blue-eyed grass are found in meadows and fields across Canada.

NOTES: The specific name *angustifolium*, 'narrow-leaved', refers to the foliage of this plant.

Blue Camas

Camassia quamash
LILIACEAE (LILY FAMILY)

Camas flowers wash meadows a startling blue-violet each spring. Towering above the grass-like leaves is a loose cluster of wheel-shaped flowers punctuated with yellow anthers. The vivid blooms of this perennial attract a number of insects, like the bee in this photograph. A similar but more robust species, great camas (*Camassia leichlinii*), blooms a few weeks later.

HABITAT/RANGE: Although most abundant in the west, several species of camas are found in the moist soils of open meadows across Canada. Wild hyacinth (*C. scilloides*), a similar eastern species, occurs in southern Ontario.

NOTES: Camas was a staple food of the Coast and Plains Indians. The large glutinous bulbs were dug up during or just after flowering and then steam-cooked in large pits.

Western Buttercup

Ranunculus occidentalis
RANUNCULACEAE (BUTTERCUP
FAMILY)

The sheen and brilliance of buttercup petals is produced by a layer of wax on the upper surface and the oil-flled epidermal cells. When an insect lands on the flower, it reaches down to the base of the petal where the nectar is stored in a little scale. Each plant blooms for four to nine days, opening its petals between eight and ten o'clock in the morning and closing them between three and six in the afternoon.

HABITAT/RANGE: With over forty species represented across North America, the buttercup is one of our most common wildflowers. Western buttercup is restricted to western Canada.

NOTES: The generic name *Ranunculus*, 'little frog', may refer to the fact that many buttercups grow in moist areas.

California Poppy

Eschscholzia californica

PAPAVERACEAE (POPPY FAMILY)

California poppies add a festive air to coastal meadows from March to September. Each stalk bears a single flower displaying four large fan-shaped petals and a conspicuous pink rim at the base of the ovary. Beetles attracted to the brilliant colour and spicy scent of the blooms serve as pollinators. Thought to be very sensitive to sunlight, the flowers remain closed at night and on cloudy days, when the plant can be recognized by its fern-like bluish-green foliage.

HABITAT/RANGE: Escaped from gardens, California poppy is now abundant in fields and meadows along the drier southern coast of British Columbia.

NOTES: This poppy is the state flower of California, where masses of blooms paint the hillsides a brilliant tangerine hue.

Prairie Buttercup

Ranunculus rhomboideus
RANUNCULACEAE (BUTTERCUP
FAMILY)

Flowering in early May, this perennial en-
livens open areas with its five light yellow
petals and shorter golden and lavender-
tinged sepals. The leaves are spoon-shaped
with wavy margins, while the stem leaves
are stalkless and deeply divided.

HABITAT/RANGE: The prairie species is one
of the most common buttercups on the plains,
occurring in dry grasslands and parklands
throughout most of the prairie provinces.

NOTES: Botanists consider buttercups to be
among the most primitive of flowering-
plant families. One reason for their long
survival is that buttercups' reproductive
structures are not only attractive but easily
accessible to a wide variety of pollinating
insects. At the base of each of the five waxy
yellow petals is a sweet-scented nectary that
invites both short-tongued honeybees and
long-tongued bumblebees, butterflies, and
moths. As these insects feed on the nectar
they are likely to brush against some of the
buttercup's numerous pistils and stamens,
pollinating the flower in the process.

Upland Larkspur

Delphinium nuttalianum
RANUNCULACEAE (BUTTERCUP FAMILY)

The blue-purple flowers of upland larkspur bloom in early summer. A characteristic feature of larkspur flowers is the long, conspicuous spur formed by the upper sepal and uppermost pair of petals. This contains the nectar, which is accessible only to butterflies and long-proboscis bumblebees. Upland larkspur's flower stalks and deeply lobed basal leaves are covered with fine hairs, giving this perennial a woolly, greyish appearance.

HABITAT/RANGE: A number of larkspur species range throughout western Canada. Upland larkspur favours sagebrush desert or open ponderosa pine woods, notably in southern British Columbia and Alberta.

NOTES: The leaves of larkspur contain delphinine, a toxic alkaloid known to cause extreme sickness or death in cattle. Sheep, which are not affected by the poison, have been used to eliminate larkspurs from cattle ranges.

Queen Anne's Lace

Daucus carota

UMBELLIFERAE (PARSLEY FAMILY)

Along roadsides across Canada, the blooms of Queen Anne's lace sway gently in the warm breezes of summer. A closer look at the flat-topped cluster reveals that it is actually composed of hundreds of tiny white flowers grouped together. Each flower has five irregularly shaped petals, five thread-like stamens, and two small styles. In the centre of some umbels is a small dark purple flower that is sterile and may serve as a landing platform to attract insects. After the flowers have been pollinated and the seeds begin to mature, the umbel curls in on itself, giving rise to another common name for the plant: bird's nest.

HABITAT/RANGE: This introduced species is found in fields and waste places across Canada.

NOTES: Also known as wild carrot, Queen Anne's lace has finely-cut leaves resembling carrot tops and seeds with a strong carrot taste.

Wild Parsnip

Pastinaca sativa

UMBELLIFERAE (PARSLEY FAMILY)

This wild version of the cultivated parsnip has a stout, deeply grooved stem, numerous sharply toothed leaflets, and a large yellow flower head, known as an umbel, that makes an attractive, accessible target for insects. Each tiny individual flower offers nectar exposed on the flat disk surrounding the base of the pistil.

HABITAT/RANGE: Wild parsnip grows along roadsides and in waste places, particularly in eastern and central Canada.

NOTES: Botanists have determined that more insects visit clustered flower heads like those in the parsley and composite families than the flowers of other plant families. The spider in this photograph is waiting to prey on one of the many insects that feed on wild parsnip flowers.

Alpine Tundra

Alpine tundra is found in areas where the climate is too cold and the growing season too short for normal tree growth. To reach these harsh environs you can travel either north or up—if you're climbing a mountain trail, for instance, every 200-metre gain in altitude is the equivalent of walking more than 260 kilometres towards the north pole, and results in a one-degree drop in the mean temperature. In southern Canada the alpine tundra is most prevalent in the western mountains, where it is encountered at altitudes of 1,500 to 2,000 metres. Although there is little mountain terrain in eastern Canada high enough to limit the growth of trees, small regions of tundra do occur on the Gaspé Peninsula. You reach the tree line at progressively lower altitudes as you travel north. The true arctic begins where the climate is too cold even at sea level for trees to grow. Despite the great distance between the tundra of the southern Rockies and that of the Arctic, the plant communities of the two regions are closely related and have developed special mechanisms and behaviours to cope with the extreme conditions of their icy habitat.

The short growing season of the alpine tundra regions demands that plants take full advantage of the limited sunlight. In the few fleeting weeks of summer they must not only grow and manufacture and store food, but develop flowers, seeds, and fruit. After the long period of winter dormancy, most tundra flowers will burst from the ground even before the snow has melted.

The harsh conditions favour perennials like glacier lily and western anemone, whose initial period of rapid growth is fuelled with energy stored in their underground root stocks rather than manufactured in their leaves. The brightly coloured blossoms of lupines, arnicas, and monkey flowers absorb sunlight readily and are several degrees warmer than white-petalled varieties, allowing for greater nectar production and faster seed development.

The obvious pattern of tundra growth is, again, largely a function of temperature: the higher the elevation or more northerly the latitude, the more dwarfed the plant life. Despite the cold and the bitter winds, plants must stay warm enough to carry out photosynthesis, which generally ceases at temperatures of less than 5°C. To conserve heat by escaping wind chill, most species hug the ground. Arctic willow is dwarfed: a fifty-year-old tree may be no more than ankle-high. The dense, low-lying, sheltering cushions formed by some plants create micro-zones with temperatures considerably higher than their surroundings. Although some tundra species can be frozen stiff and continue to grow after thawing out, many have special features to retain both heat and moisture: a coat of insulating hairs, a thick epidermal layer, or, in the case of Labrador tea, leaf edges that are rolled under, to deflect wind from the surface.

Tundra habitats are often not only cold but dry. Many plants must be capable of absorbing and retaining the moisture available from the brief period of spring melting. Some saxifrages, for example, have fleshy, succulent leaves that permit them to survive the drought-like conditions resulting from sparse soils and rapid run-off. Many plants have adapted to the thin layer of soil above the permanently frozen ground by putting down short, dense networks of roots.

The rapid production of vegetation demanded by the short growing season attracts a variety of herbivores to the alpine tundra. Many have migrational patterns that capitalize on the verdancy of this vegetation zone. Black and grizzly bears gorge on sweet blueberries and huckleberries, while elk, deer, and caribou browse on the lush foliage of lilies and lupines. Insects and even hummingbirds fly up to the alpine meadows, attracted by the vivid colour and sweet nectar of plants like columbine and Indian paintbrush.

Mountain Valerian

Valeriana sitchensis
VALERIANACEAE (VALERIAN
FAMILY)

Mountain valerian is one of the most fragrant of alpine flowers. Crowning the tall
squared stem is an open cluster of small,
five-petalled blossoms that over the summer
fade from lavender-pink to white. A lush
perennial, this plant has three to five dark
green toothed leaflets.

HABITAT/RANGE: Mountain valerian
thrives in rich moist soils in subalpine forests across British Columbia and into
Alberta.

NOTES: The thick root-stocks of mountain
valerian, which have a disagreeable odour,
were eaten by the Plains Indians as a remedy
for stomach ailments.

Alpine Willow-Herb

Epilobium alpinum

ONAGRACEAE (EVENING PRIMROSE
FAMILY)

Willow-herb, or alpine fireweed, is a low
shrubby plant that is common along mountain streams. From its bent, leafy stems
grow several small, pink or purplish flowers. The blooms, which are only about half
a centimetre long, display four sepals, four
petals, eight stamens, and one pistil. After
the petals wither, the flowers mature into
long, slender seed pods which are characteristic of willow-herb. Alpine willow-
herb's narrow, alternate leaves, which resemble those of a willow, give rise to its
common name.

HABITAT/RANGE: Alpine willow-herb
thrives in moist conditions near streams or
wet, rocky outcrops in the high alpine.

NOTES: Fireweed is transcontinental in its
range, flourishing in the far north, where
common fireweed is the official emblem of
the Yukon territory.

Elephant's Head

Pedicularis groenlandica
SCROPHULARIACEAE (FIGWORT
FAMILY)

Tall spikes of tightly packed reddish-purple
flowers blooming in midsummer and an
abundance of fringed leaves near the base of
the plant distinguish this member of the
figwort family. As the common name implies, each flower resembles an elephant's
head, complete with ears and a raised trunk.

HABITAT/RANGE: Elephant's head is found
along alpine streams and in moist mountain
meadows throughout western Canada. Similar species in the genus *Pedicularis* occur in
the arctic.

NOTES: Even when elephant's head is not in
bloom, its maroon-tinged stem and leaves
make it one of the most conspicuous Rocky
Mountain species.

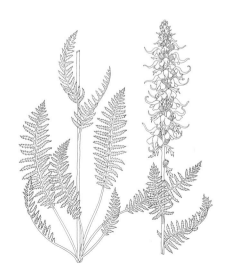

White Moss Heather

Cassiope mertensiana
ERICACEAE (HEATH FAMILY)

The dainty bell-shaped flowers of white moss heather nod among the alpine rocks in early summer. Equally distinctive is the cord-like evergreen foliage: four rows of scaly leaves pressed so close together that they resemble twigs or pipe-cleaners. Like other alpine flora, white moss heather grows very slowly. In most cases, the cold temperatures and bitter winds limit its size to that of a ground-hugging shrub.

HABITAT/RANGE: White moss heather is one of the most common shrubs above the timber-line. Its range is restricted to alpine regions of western Canada, although similar species are found in the arctic tundra.

NOTES: White moss heather is often confused with white mountain heather (*Cassiope tetragona*). Otherwise very similar in appearance, the latter is distinguished by the deep grooves on the lower surface of its leaves.

Red Monkey Flower

Mimulus lewisii

SCROPHULARIACEAE (FIGWORT FAMILY)

Masses of red monkey flower bloom throughout July and August in moist alpine meadows. One of Canada's showiest alpine blossoms, it resembles a snapdragon with a two-lobed upper lip and a three-lobed lower one. To attract pollinators, the hairy throat is marked with a deep yellow. The whole plant is covered with sticky hairs, including the conspicuously veined opposite leaves.

HABITAT/RANGE: Red monkey flower thrives in wet alpine areas, usually along stream banks and on gentle slopes where there is considerable seepage from melting snow. Its range is restricted to western Canada.

NOTES: The deep pink to crimson flowers attract various hummingbird species into the mountains during the brief summer blooming period.

Wild Tiger Lily

Lilium columbianum

LILIACEAE (LILY FAMILY)

Wild tiger lily is striking both in its size and in its spectacular nodding blossom. A vigorous perennial, it can reach a metre in height and produce as many as thirty flowers in one summer. The bloom consists of six reflexed orange tepals, speckled with maroon, surrounding a spray of dangling anthers. Narrow lance-shaped leaves grow in whorls up the long stem.

HABITAT/RANGE: Wild tiger lily ranges across southern British Columbia to the Rockies. Although more common at lower elevations, it does occur in subalpine meadows.

NOTES: Deer, elk, mountain sheep, and mountain goats all browse on wild tiger lily.

◁ A black-tailed deer enjoys a stalk of tiger lily.

Fireweed

Epilobium angustifolium
ONAGRACEAE (EVENING PRIMROSE FAMILY)

Growing in dense clusters, fireweed is one of the first plants to invade clearings and burned-over areas. Its long lance-shaped leaves grow alternately up the tall stem, which is crowned by a pink flowering spike. Blooming progressively from the bottom up, the flowers mature into silky winged seeds that are dispersed by the autumn breezes.

HABITAT/RANGE: Fireweed is common in disturbed areas across most of Canada, ascending to well above timber-line (where it is dwarfed in stature). Its range is circumboreal but not arctic.

NOTES: Nectar production in fireweed flowers reaches a peak shortly after high noon, when bees swarm over the plants. Fireweed honey is prized for its fragrance and taste.

Broad-leaved Lupine

Lupinus arcticus
LEGUMINOSAE (PEA FAMILY)

The deep azure of flowering lupines has enlivened the trek of many a tired hiker. This tufted perennial displays fan-like whorls of leaflets and the typical pea flower. The uppermost petal is called the standard, the two side petals are the wings, and the bottom edges of the lower two petals are fused together into the boat-shaped keel, which cradles the stamens and pistil. When the wings and keel are pushed down by an insect, the stamens act as a piston forcing out a ribbon of pollen from a small hole at the tip of the keel onto the underside of the visiting insect.

HABITAT/RANGE: Broad-leaved lupine occurs on grassy alpine slopes throughout British Columbia, the Yukon, and Alberta. Many other lupine species are found across Canada.

NOTES: Like other members of the pea family, lupines have nitrogen-fixing bacteria in their roots that convert nitrogen from the air into soil nitrates, which are used for plant growth.

Small-flowered Paintbrush

Castilleja parviflora
SCROPHULARIACEAE (FIGWORT FAMILY)

Although similar in form to red Indian paintbrush, the small-flowered species is much shorter. The flower bracts, which vary from rose-coloured to crimson to creamy-white, partially conceal the actual flowers. Woolly hairs coat the slim, un-branched stems and alternate leaves, giving this perennial a soft, downy appearance.

HABITAT/RANGE: Small-flowered paint-brush occurs in mountainous regions throughout most of British Columbia and in the Rockies in Alberta.

NOTES: Although most Indian paintbrushes are bright red, there are a few yellow and cream-coloured species. This large genus is found primarily in western Canada.

Tall Purple Fleabane

Erigeron peregrinus
COMPOSITAE (COMPOSITE FAMILY)

The large, daisy-like flower heads of tall purple fleabane enliven alpine meadows throughout the summer. Rising from a loose basal tuft of lance-shaped leaves, this tall perennial can reach 60 centimetres in height. Together, the numerous ray florets, which are toothed at the tip and may be purple, pink, or white, and the yellow disks attract a variety of insects; the one in the photograph is a skipper butterfly.

HABITAT/RANGE: Tall purple fleabane is common in alpine regions, ranging across British Columbia into the Rocky Mountains. Similar species are found in the arctic tundra.

NOTES: The peculiar name fleabane originated in the belief that these plants could repel fleas.

Tall Brook Ragwort

Senecio triangularis
COMPOSITAE (COMPOSITE FAMILY)

Were it not for its long triangular leaves and smooth, shiny stems, this coarse perennial could easily be mistaken for marsh ragwort. Tall brook ragwort has long leafy stems topped by branched clusters of yellow flowers. The small, daisy-like flower heads are encircled by a ring of bracts that protect the flowers as they mature. The eight yellow rays produced by most flowers add a splash of colour to the end-of-summer blooming period and continue to attract insect pollinators even after the petals begin to drop off.

HABITAT/RANGE: Many different ragwort species are found across Canada in meadow habitats. Tall brook ragwort thrives along stream banks and in moist meadows in the alpine regions of western Canada.

NOTES: Ragworts are members of the largest family of flowering plants, the composites.

◁ Tall brook ragwort, paintbrush, and lupine fill an alpine meadow.

Mountain Veronica

Veronica alpina
SCROPHULARIACEAE (FIGWORT FAMILY)

This dainty perennial brightens mountain meadows in July and August with its loose cluster of deep violet-blue blooms. At first glance all four petals seem to be of equal size, but closer examination reveals that the upper petal is wider than the other three. Protruding beyond the petals are the stamens and pistil. The small, somewhat oval leaves are arranged in opposite pairs up the slender, hairy stem.

HABITAT/RANGE: Mountain veronica is found at moderate to high elevations throughout British Columbia and the Yukon and is locally abundant in the Rocky Mountains.

NOTES: Also known as alpine speedwell, this is one of a small group of low-growing plants in the figwort family. They are characterized by weak stems, dark green foliage, and small blue flowers.

Wood Betony

Pedicularis bracteosa
SCROPHULARIACEAE (FIGWORT FAMILY)

The flowers of wood betony display the curious beak that is characteristic of the lousewort, or *Pedicularis*, genus. Blooming in midsummer on a clustered spike, each pinkish-yellow flower consists of a long, hooded upper lip and a shorter, three-lobed lower one. A tall perennial, wood betony is also known as northern fernleaf because of its fringed foliage. The finely divided leaves can be bronzed or purplish in colour.

HABITAT/RANGE: Wood betony thrives in open woods and wet meadows in alpine regions throughout southern British Columbia and Alberta.

NOTES: The generic name *Pedicularis*, 'little louse', alludes to the superstition that livestock eating these plants would be infested by lice.

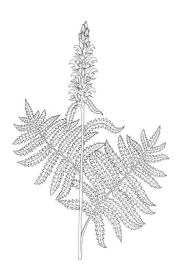

Red Indian Paintbrush

Castilleja miniata
SCROPHULARIACEAE (FIGWORT FAMILY)

Red Indian paintbrush is one of the most familiar and vivid of alpine flowers. A perennial, it is crowned by the cluster of bright red, leaf-like bracts sheltering the less conspicuous tubular green flowers. Growing alternately from the hairy stem are narrow, lance-shaped leaves with fuzzy surfaces.

HABITAT/RANGE: Red Indian paintbrush is widespread in alpine regions throughout western Canada, favouring moist meadows. Many other species occur in this region, ranging in colour from frosty white to yellow, pink, and purple.

NOTES: Most Indian paintbrushes are partially parasitic on the roots of other plants. As a result, they need few leaves with which to manufacture food and are difficult to transplant to home gardens.

Indian Hellebore

Veratrum viride

LILIACEAE (LILY FAMILY)

The lush, thickly ribbed foliage of Indian hellebore lends an almost tropical flavour to alpine meadows. Reaching a height of 1.5 metres, this robust perennial towers dramatically over neighbouring flora. The large clasping leaves are much more impressive than the pale greenish-yellow flowers. These thin branching tassels bloom throughout the summer.

HABITAT/RANGE: Indian hellebore is found in damp woods and moist meadows across most of southern Canada, including alpine regions.

NOTES: Beware of the thick root-stocks and leaves of Indian hellebore — they are violently poisonous. This plant is also commonly called green or false hellebore.

Alpine Forget-me-not

Myosotis alpestris
BORAGINACEAE (BORAGE
FAMILY)

In summer the fragrant blooms of alpine forget-me-not transform mountain meadows into an unforgettable sea of blue. Each flower has five petals and a bright yellow centre of five stamens and one pistil. The soft, narrow leaves grow alternately up the slender stem.

HABITAT/RANGE: Forget-me-nots bloom across Canada. This alpine species is restricted to mountain meadows throughout southern British Columbia and the Rocky Mountains in Alberta.

NOTES: With the aid of a hand lens you can see the distinctly hooked tips of some of the hairs on the calyx — a good identifying feature of alpine forget-me-not.

Spreading Phlox

Phlox diffusa
POLEMONICAEAE (PHLOX FAMILY)

This low-lying perennial opens its showy, fragrant flowers in the warm sun of mid-summer. Pale pink in this photograph, the flowers can vary in colour from white through pink to various shades of purple. Requiring little soil or water, spreading phlox can survive along dry ridges and rock faces. The small, narrow leaves, which grow opposite one another on the short stems, add to its dwarfed appearance. By reducing surface area, this mat-like growth form also reduces the water loss that results from the constant winds.

HABITAT/RANGE: Spreading phlox ranges throughout the mountains of British Columbia. Similar species are found in the prairie provinces.

NOTES: Spreading phlox has its stamens at different levels inside the corolla tube, to ensure that insects of various sizes will be dusted with pollen as they visit the nectar reservoir.

Western Anemone

Anemone occidentalis
RANUNCULACEAE (BUTTERCUP FAMILY)

One of the first alpine flowers to bloom, western anemone pokes its large cup-shaped flowers out of the ground soon after the snow melts. The showy blooms have five or six white sepals instead of petals. After the sepals have blown away and the fruits begin to develop, a large fluffy seed head develops on the elongated flowering stalk. This hardy perennial is distinguished by its hairy stem and finely divided leaves.

HABITAT/RANGE: Western anemone is found in moist alpine meadows and on grassy slopes in mountain ranges across British Columbia and in high altitudes in the Rockies.

NOTES: Western anemone is also commonly named towhead baby or wind flower, because of its seed head, as shown in this photograph. Chilly alpine winds disperse the silky seeds.

A blue grouse finds shelter among lupines and mountain hairgrass.

Globeflower

Trollius laxus
RANUNCULACEAE (BUTTERCUP
FAMILY)

The bowl-shaped blooms of globeflower appear as soon as the snow melts. Lacking petals, each flower has five to ten large white sepals surrounding numerous yellow stamens. The smooth leaves, jaggedly cut into five or more lobes, resemble those of buttercups.

HABITAT/RANGE: Globeflower is found, often in abundance, in moist alpine meadows near streams in British Columbia and Alberta.

NOTES: The outermost ring of modified, tubular-lipped stamens may be a source of nectar for butterflies and other insects, which have been observed foraging around the anthers.

146

Red Mountain Heather

Phyllodoce empetriformis
ERICACEAE (HEATH FAMILY)

Red heather carpets slopes above timber-line with its short, needle-like leaves. The stiff foliage and numerous branches lend a matted appearance to this low-lying evergreen shrub. Its nodding, bell-shaped rose-pink blooms brighten and perfume the alpine slopes in midsummer.

HABITAT/RANGE: Red mountain heather thrives from timber-line to the high alpine regions of British Columbia, extending into the eastern slopes of the Rockies and north into the Yukon.

NOTES: Of similar habitat and range is yellow mountain heather (*Phyllodoce glanduliflora*). It resembles red mountain heather except for its urn-shaped creamy-yellow flowers and lighter green leaves. Where the two species grow together, a pale pink-flowered hybrid often occurs.

Tolmie's Saxifrage

Saxifraga tolmiei
SAXIFRAGACEAE (SAXIFRAGE FAMILY)

This tiny inhabitant of high rock ridges, also known as alpine saxifrage, is distinguished by a succulent mat of small evergreen leaves. The thick, round-tipped leaves store water, helping the plant to survive long periods of drought when the thin soil freezes. One or more star-like white flowers crown the short flower stalk. Each flower has five petals and generally ten stamens. The fruit matures into a capsule with two styles.

HABITAT/RANGE: A number of saxifrage species, all rock-dwellers, are found in alpine and arctic tundra regions. Tolmie's saxifrage grows on rocky ledges in mountainous areas across British Columbia.

NOTES: The generic name *Saxifraga* comes from the Latin *saxum*, 'rock', and *frangare*, 'to break'. It probably alludes to the rock-cleaving properties of the saxifrage root system.

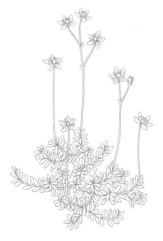

Glacier Lily

Erythronium grandiflorum
LILIACEAE (LILY FAMILY)

Nodding farewell to winter, the pure yellow flowers of glacier lily emerge soon after the snow melts. Each plant bears between one and five graceful blossoms consisting of six recurved petals and a pair of glossy green oval leaves. Glacier lily usually occurs with western anemone and spring beauty in the first wave of alpine blooms.

HABITAT/RANGE: Glacier lily grows along brooks and in alpine meadows across southern British Columbia and Alberta.

NOTES: The bulbs of glacier lily are dug up and eaten by small rodents as well as black and grizzly bears, which move up to the mountains during the summer. Mule deer will browse on the leaves and eat the large immature seed pods.

Alpine Arnica
Arnica angustifolia
COMPOSITAE (COMPOSITE FAMILY)

Look for the golden blooms of alpine arnica on high rock ridges throughout the summer. This hardy perennial usually has one large flower head displaying between nine and twelve notched rays. The lance-shaped leaves grow in opposite pairs on the woolly stem. Almost the entire plant is covered with little hairs — a common feature of alpine flora. The hairs help to conserve water by limiting air flow over the surface of the plant.

HABITAT/RANGE: Alpine arnica occurs in alpine areas throughout western Canada, as well as in the arctic. It varies in form, becoming smaller as elevation increases or temperature decreases.

NOTES: The name arnica is derived from the Greek *arnakis*, 'lamb's skin', and refers to the woolly bracts at the base of the flowers.

Columbian ground squirrels take advantage of the abundance of alpine herbs available during the fleeting growing season. ▷

Glossary

Alternate: of leaves, growing singly up a stem, not in pairs.

Annual: a plant that lives for only one year or growing season.

Anther: the enlarged, pollen-bearing tip of the stamen.

Basal: referring to the base or lower part of a plant.

Biennial: a plant that lives for only two years, usually producing flowers and fruit the second year.

Blade: the flat surface of a leaf.

Bract: a modified leaf, usually scale-like on a stem and petal-like on a flower.

Bulb: a swollen underground bud consisting of fleshy, food-storing leaves attached to the base of a stem.

Calyx: the collective name for the sepals of a flower.

Cluster: a number of flowers or fruits grouped together.

Column: a structure formed by the union of stamens and pistils in an orchid.

Compound (or divided): of a leaf, composed of two or more leaflets with a common stalk.

Conifer: a cone-bearing tree such as a pine, fir, or spruce.

Corolla: the collective name for the petals of a flower.

Cross-pollination: the process in which pollen from one plant is transferred to the stigma of another plant.

Deciduous: having leaves that are shed every year.

Disk florets: the small tubular flowers located at the centre of a composite flower head.

Divided: see compound.

Entire: of a leaf, having an even and unbroken margin.

Evergreen: a plant that retains its green leaves throughout the year.

Family: a group of related genera.

Filament: the thin stalk that supports the anther.

Floret: a small flower that is part of a large cluster.

Flower: the part of the plant that contains the male and/or female reproductive parts.

Flower head: a grouping of many small flowers into one bunch at the top of a stem.

Flowering plant: any plant that produces true flowers bearing seeds enclosed in a fruit.

Fruit: the matured ovary containing the seeds.

Genus: a group of closely related species.

Herb: a non-woody plant.

Irregular flower: a flower in which the sepals and petals are not all the same size or shape, such as an orchid or violet.

Keel: the two partly fused lower petals of many flowers in the pea family.

Leaf: a plant organ whose main function is to absorb sunlight energy to combine carbon dioxide and water into carbohydrates, through the process of photosynthesis.

Leaflet: a single division of a compound leaf (e.g., a clover has three leaflets).

Lip: a protruding, elongated basal petal occurring in an irregular flower.

Lobed: referring to leaves that are deeply cut into prominent projections.

Nectar: the sweet fluid produced by a flower to attract insects or other pollinators.

Opposite: of leaves, growing in pairs opposite each other on a stem.

Ovary: the swollen lower part of a pistil that contains the egg cells that develop into seeds.

Perennial: a plant that lives for two or more years.

Perfect flowers: a flower with functional stamens and pistils.

Petal: one of the colourful inner leaf-like structures surrounding the reproductive parts of a flower.

Petiole: the stalk supporting the leaf.

Pinnately divided: referring to a divided or compound leaf in which the leaflets grow in a feather-like arrangement on opposite sides of an elongated axis.

Pistil: the female reproductive structure of a flower, consisting of the ovary, style, and stigma.

Pollen: the dusty yellow substance, produced by the anthers, that contains the male sex cells.

Raceme: a long cluster of flowers arranged singly along a stalk.

Ray floret: the individual petal-like flowers that surround the centre (made up of disk florets) of a composite flower head.

Rhizome: a creeping underground stem that stores food and is a means of vegetative reproduction.

Roots: the underground parts of a plant that anchor the stem and absorb water and nutrients.

Rosette: a dense ring of basal leaves.

Seed: a reproductive structure consisting of a small embryonic plant and food storage tissue, enclosed in a seed coat.

Sepals: the outer leaf-like parts of a flower that enclose the flower in the bud stage.

Shrub: a small woody perennial with several stems.

Spadix: a club-like stalk of tiny, tightly clustered flowers.

Spathe: a hood-like leafy sheath enclosing the spadix (e.g., the yellow cloak of skunk cabbage).

Species: the smallest category of classification whose members are very much alike.

Spike: a long flower cluster with densely packed stalkless flowers.

Spur: a slender, hollow extension of a petal; often a nectar receptacle.

Stamen: the male reproductive part, consisting of the filament and anther.

Stem: the part of the plant above the root that supports the leaves and flowers.

Stigma: the tip of the pistil that receives the pollen.

Stipule: one of a pair of leaf-like appendages at the base of a petiole.

Style: the part of the pistil that connects the ovary and the stigma.

Tap root: the large central root of a plant that grows straight down into the soil.

Tepal: a term used for sepals and petals that are so similar in colour and shape that they cannot be easily distinguished.

Terminal: growing at the end of a stem or branch.

Umbel: a flat-topped, umbrella-like flower cluster in which all flower stalks radiate from a single point.

Whorl: three or more leaves radiating from a common point in a wheel-like arrangement.

Selected References

Bailey, L.H. *How Plants Get Their Names.* New York: Dover, 1933.

Clark, L.J., 1976. *Wild Flowers of the Pacific Northwest from Alaska to Northern California.* Sidney, B.C.: Gray's Publishing, 1976.

Cormack, R.G.H. *Wild Flowers of Alberta.* Edmonton: Hurtig, 1977.

Ferguson, M., and R. Saunders. *Canadian Wildflowers.* Toronto: Van Nostrand Reinhold, 1976.

Hitchcock, C.L. and A. Cronquist. *Flora of the Pacific Northwest: An Illustrated Manual.* Seattle: University of Washington Press, 1973.

Hosie, R.C. *Native Trees of Canada.* Don Mills, Ont.: Fitzhenry and Whiteside, 1979.

Kozloff, E.N. *Plants and Animals of the Pacific Northwest: An Illustrated Guide to the Natural History of Western Oregon, Washington, and British Columbia.* Seattle: University of Washington Press, 1976.

Looman, J. and K.F. Best. *Budd's Flora of the Canadian Prairie Provinces.* Ottawa: Minister of Supply and Services, 1979.

Lyons, C.P. *Trees, Shrubs and Flowers to know in British Columbia.* Toronto: J.M. Dent, 1974.

Mackenzie, K. *Wildflowers of Eastern Canada — Ontario, Quebec and Atlantic Provinces.* Toronto and Montreal: Tundra Books of Montreal and Collins, 1973.

Martin, A.C., H.S. Zim, and A.L. Nelson. *American Wildlife and Plants: A Guide to Wildlife Food Habits.* New York: Dover, 1961.

Newcomb, L. *Newcomb's Wildflower Guide.* Boston: Little, Brown, 1977.

Peterson, L. *A Field Guide to Edible Plants of Eastern and Central North America.* Boston: Houghton Mifflin, 1978.

Peterson, R.T., and M. McKenny. *A Field Guide to Wildflowers of Northeastern and Northcentral North America.* Boston: Houghton Mifflin, 1968.

Porsild, A.E. *Rocky Mountain Wildflowers.* Ottawa: National Museum of Natural Sciences, 1979.

Scoggan, H.J. *The Flora of Canada.* 4 vols. Ottawa: National Museum of Natural Sciences, 1978.

Spellenberg, R. *The Audubon Society Field Guide to North American Wildflowers: Western Region.* New York: Knopf, 1979.

Stokes, D.W. *A Guide to Observing Insect Lives.* Boston: Little, Brown, 1983.

Stokes, D.W. and L.Q. *A Guide to Enjoying Wildflowers.* Boston: Little, Brown, 1985.

Trelawny, J.G. *Wildflowers of the Yukon and Northwestern Canada including adjacent Alaska.* Sidney, B.C.: Gray's Publishing, 1983.

Turner, N.J. *Food Plants of British Columbia Indians, Part 1/Coastal Peoples.* British Columbia Museum Handbook 34. Victoria: British Columbia Provincial Museum, 1975.

Turner, N.J., and A.F. Szczawinski. *Edible Wild Plants of Canada,* Nos. 1, 2, 3, 4. Ottawa: National Museum of Natural Sciences, 1978.

Underhill, J.E., and C.C. Chuang. *Wildflowers of Manning Park.* Victoria: British Columbia Parks Branch and British Columbia Provincial Museum, 1976.

Vance, F.R., J.R. Jowsey, and J.S. McLean, *Wildflowers Across the Prairies.* Saskatoon: Western Producer Prairie Books, 1977.

Ward-Harris, J. *More Than Meets the Eye: The Life and Lore of Western Wildflowers.* Toronto: Oxford University Press Canada, 1983.

Zichmanis, J., and J. Hodgins. *Flowers of the Wild — Ontario and the Great Lakes Region.* Toronto: Oxford University Press Canada, 1982.

Index of Common Names

Index of Scientific Names